TEACHER to TEACHER

Learning from Each Other

The Experienced Teachers Group

Herbert H. "Burry" Gowen II

Duane Grobman II

Tracey Guth

Rosario Jaramillo

Douglas Jones

Jane Kays

Susan McCray

Jorge Mejia

Kristin Newton

Suzy Ort

Mark Schoeffel

Christopher Whitbeck

Elissa Wolf

Teacher to Teacher

Learning from Each Other

Eleanor Duckworth
and the Experienced Teachers Group

TEACHERS
COLLEGE
PRESS

Teachers College
Columbia University
New York and London

In memory of Soraya Cordoba, half the royalties from the sale of this book will be given to the Anexo San Francisco de Asis, a school for barrio children in Bogota, Colombia.

Published by Teachers College Press, 1234 Amsterdam Avenue, New York, NY 10027

Library of Congress Cataloging-in-Publication Data

Duckworth, Eleanor Ruth.
    Teacher to teacher : learning from each other / Eleanor Duckworth and the Experienced Teachers Group.
        p.   cm.
    Includes bibliographical references and index.
    ISBN 0-8077-3653-8 (cloth). — ISBN 0-8077-3652-X (pbk.)
    1. Teaching — United States.   2. Teachers — In-service training —
United States.   3. Experienced Teachers Group.   I. Experienced
Teachers Group.   II. Title.
    LB1025.3.D847   1997
    371.102 — dc21   97-20976

ISBN 0-8077-3652-X (paper)
ISBN 0-8077-3653-8 (cloth)

Printed on acid-free paper
Manufactured in the United States of America

04   03   02   01   00   99   98   8   7   6   5   4   3   2

Contents

v

Foreword

I write this foreword from a perspective that is at once nostalgic and critical. As a colleague or instructor of most of the book's authors, I began reading *Teacher to Teacher: Learning from Each Other* enviously. Good memories were called up as I read the authors' accounts of their collaborative work thinking through the thorny issues in education. Satisfaction replaced envy, however, a few pages into reading this book as wonderful insights and well-told stories conveyed an essence of fourteen teachers talking among themselves. Readers of this book have a good seat in the audience, an engaging one.

Most of *Teacher to Teacher*, a collection of essays, discussions, and journal entries, engages us as wonderful conversation: We become brighter and more interesting ourselves, as a result of being involved as readers. Moreover, the book extends itself, inviting passionate conversation on a multitude of ideas about learning, ideas that advance our understanding of what it means to try to teach children in American schools at the end of the twentieth century. This is a rare book that is good to share with a friend, a colleague, a reading group, a class.

Appearing at a time when reforming educational practice is widely debated, *Teacher to Teacher* has a wide appeal; teachers and others active in schools will be drawn to its multiple approaches to classroom education. The authors' experiences in the classroom are varied, instructive, and fluently told. People who work outside these environments will get a sense of why any single educational question produces passionate debate. Conversations among teachers from different kinds of schools—public schools, independent schools, elementary, junior high, high, affluent, poor, rural, urban, suburban schools—are enriched by a pervasive question: How much can we learn from each other? Under what circumstances can experience gained in one classroom be useful in another?

When teachers clear time to ponder such questions, and to articulate, argue, and publish, there is, in Eleanor Duckworth's justly renowned phrase, "the having of wonderful ideas." *Teacher to Teacher* multiplies these wonders; its distinctive composition is a collage of various approaches to questions. It offers multiple approaches to learning about schools, and it invites multiple approaches to reading. Let me mention just three.

Teacher to Teacher might first be approached straightforwardly. To learn about schools we go to a firsthand account of what fourteen insiders say matters about classroom learning: descriptions of classrooms, human dilemmas, children, assessment practices, life circumstances – that is, the tangibles composing educational quality, and the essentials of learning and instructing. In so doing, we get stories of schools and talk about schools as well as proposals for reform. Reform is the daily business of teachers. "How can we do this better?" is the question readers will infer from almost every page. So our straightforward reading of "insider" stories includes readers in the dialogue.

A second approach to *Teacher to Teacher* views the book as a documentary on the processes involved when teachers struggle to talk about their craft. These processes are fascinating in themselves. In particular, the group effort to organize a learning forum free from traditional restraints is instructive. We read how moments of dazzling insight alternate with reflections on missed opportunities. It is also worth paying close attention to the process discussions in the book, for the reflection to which these professionals commit themselves is one that requires self-discipline. And self-discipline is so often obscured and eroded by the institutions in which professionals operate. But this book tells another story, too. It tells about what happens when teachers work under circumstances that might be considered ideal, with few bureaucratic demands and a small group of dedicated colleagues. It tells precisely *how*, even here, time still gets wasted and people are still marginalized at important moments. Two exceptional features of this book are its honesty and its completeness. The documentarians' readings of *Teacher to Teacher* will begin to piece together how it is that teacher colleagues learn from each other. Readers who want to promote professional dialogue will find this book a valuable roadmap of a tour once taken.

A third approach to reading *Teacher to Teacher*, one that also profits by the structure of the book, is the time-honored "compare and contrast" approach. Comparison of the views of fourteen teachers who talk about learning reveals so many approaches to their common endeavor! Diverse experience strives for overall excellence. How can we pick and choose and combine these disparate views? Each reader will decide his or her own way.

Every reader has a distinct way of reading to gain insight. And yet we have much in common. As educators, students, or parents, we inhabit cultures questing for "better" educational practices than the ones we have. This quest will continue as long as there are children to raise, things to learn, processes to evolve. Our quest is becoming sophisticated. Having largely abandoned our search for one-size-fits-all solutions, we switch from desiring pronouncements to wanting dialogue.

Part of the authority of *Teacher to Teacher* comes from its authorship by inside experts. Inside experts have much to report about the evolution of classroom practices, including about educational reform, if you will—the good stuff that can happen on the classroom level and in the details of classroom life. Insiders can answer the basic questions about classrooms: Who is in the class? What happens? What happens next? When? Were does it work best (or fail or work)? These vital details, when discussed by teachers talking to each other, give us material for consequential discussions on learning. They are authentic educational tools that can give us new opportunities to move educational discussions forward.

My own experience in teaching ethnography and collaborative inquiry in Harvard's Experienced Teachers Program led me to expect courageous insights from the authors of *Teacher to Teacher*, even before I read their work. But I underestimated how much of the texture of school life they would be able to convey. Never before has there been a book that develops so clearly the multidimensional approach to teachers learning from each other. This book breaks new ground by giving us many "takes" on questions such as: How do teachers plan their craft? How do they carry it out? How do they define obstacles? Meet them? Celebrate their victories? Come to terms with what they cannot do?

All classrooms are mysteries, obscured by the distractions of daily routines. Sometimes each of us must wonder about how classroom learning takes place at all. Indeed, we are used to cynical assertions that little learning *can* or *does* take place in schools. And yet, really, we also know that kids do learn their 3R's—and more, too—and know them better when they leave than when they begin school. In setting aside reflexive skepticism, this book illuminates the mystery of classroom learning anew.

Children spend a few hours a day in school for 180 days a year. One day they enter with a set of notions; another day, a year, a decade later, students leave with notions evolved and minds transformed by the experience, for better and for worse. But they seldom leave without having developed their academic knowledge and skills. Teachers, too, evolve their skills and abilities over the years in schools. This is a process that we understand too little, despite the widespread reports on teacher "burnout." This book's self-consciousness—the willingness to analyze a year of mutual instruction—will help readers reflect on the relationship between the way we organize kids' learning and the way we organize our own.

Educators' bookshelves are filled with books about myriad factors external to classroom life, including books about learning technologies, social problems, urban life, suburban malaise, money, disengaged parents, and social injustices. Those books are necessary for the project of reform, the eternal business of teacher. And yet, we will lose something essential and joyous if we stray too far from the classroom. *Teacher to Teacher* portrays a celebration of dedicated artists struggling and delivering. Reading it is a memorable learning experience.

Catherine G. Krupnick
Harvard University Graduate School of Education

Introduction

Eleanor Duckworth

In September of 1993, thirteen teachers joined with me in a one-year graduate program for experienced teachers. Before the end of the year, we had decided to write this book.

It is intended for teachers, for educators involved in teacher development, and for anyone interested in how teachers might think about their work. It deals with issues that concern teachers day to day and with ways that fourteen teachers devised to help themselves and each other with these issues.

One of the issues in education today is that teachers become worn out by the demands of the work. Deborah Meier (1988) has observed that there is no other work that calls so fully on a person's intellectual, interpersonal, emotional, and political resources. Teachers would and do willingly give all of that, but many leave the classroom because of the impossible professional conditions under which they are expected to work. They are too often dealt with as functionaries — meant to carry out some hierarchy's directives. The premise here, on the contrary, is that teachers, as professionals, know about education as few others do and that the field of education needs to capitalize on this knowledge.

THE EXPERIENCED TEACHERS PROGRAM

The Experienced Teachers Program (ETP) had been operating at the Harvard Graduate School of Education since the fall of 1988. Many graduate programs in education are designed to help teachers become something else — principals, organizational developers, researchers, curriculum consultants. This program was designed for teachers who wanted to become better teachers. The faculty who created this program were aware of the power of teachers who knew what they were about and who worked in concert. We wanted them to have our support in their desire to improve their craft.

Qualified teachers choose this program, and are chosen by it, once they arrive at the university in the fall. Some had applied to the program as part of their application to the graduate school. Others learned about it and indicated their interest during Orientation Week. The ETP faculty made the selection based on written statements of interest and, oddly enough, on schedules. (Work, family, or other responsibilites ruled out specific evenings for many students.) The fourteen members who ended up forming this group included nine full-time students, taking a year away from teaching; one full-time student still teaching part-time at his school; two half-time students, teaching full-time during the year; Rosario Jaramillo, a visiting scholar from Colombia (she signed on as a student/auditor, and I asked her if she would also join me in some of the planning); and myself.

The Experienced Teachers Program entailed an integrative seminar, two required courses, and three other courses to be selected within certain areas—one from the teacher's subject matter, one with a philosophical orientation, and one with an organizational orientation. Two other courses were open electives.

Required Course: Teaching and Learning (T-440)

Teaching and Learning, which I taught in the fall, is sometimes referred to in this text by its number, T-440. The purpose of the course is to help the participants to develop their own views of what it means to learn and what it means to know something, and to develop ways of teaching that are consistent with these views. It does this mainly by having people attend to themselves and each other as learners while they learn something new together. Participants are also required to find ways of engaging a variety of different students in learning some material and to pay close attention to the ways that they make sense of it as they learn. For the final 5 weeks, this work is designed by pairs of students, who are free to choose one among several proposed forms. For example, in one form, one of the students engages the other in learning some new material that the first person knows well, taking all the time necessary to explore the material in depth. In another form, the two together engage a small group of students in a similar kind of exploring. The partners also discuss the experience carefully after each session, checking out what each person felt went well, was full of interest, kept them engaged, seemed too daunting or boring, cut short some potential ideas or enthusiasm, and so on. Subject matters that have been explored have ranged from Plato's *Republic* to writing poetry, to bicycle repair, to calculus, to falling objects (see the March 3 session described later in this book).

A guiding practice throughout the course is to make sure that learners feel confident to try out their ideas, to express and explore their confusion, without fear of scoffing from a teacher or from other students who may feel they know better. My thought is that if one's knowledge is to be useful, one must feel free to examine it, to acknowledge one's confusions, and to appreciate one's own ways of seeing, of exploring, and of working through to a more satisfactory level. Curriculum planning then entails finding ways to structure subject matter so as to enable learners to get at their thoughts about it. And pedagogy entails taking those many different thoughts seriously and helping learners to pursue them in greater breadth and depth.

Required Course: Classroom Ethnography Using Visual Analysis (T-355)

Catherine Krupnick had been the major faculty member for ETP. This year, however, she was on leave in the fall, so it would not be possible for us to teach the integrative seminar together. I thought it was important nonetheless for the teachers in this program to have contact with her, and particularly with her ways of looking at classrooms. We therefore added her second semester course to the requirements for this year.

This course offers its students ways of looking at the life of classrooms and schools in order to help them think about and come to understand better how classrooms function. It asks them to be observers of intricacies and subtleties of classroom dynamics. Students look at questions such as: Who speaks, how long, how often, after whom, by invitation or as a volunteer, and with what effects? How can one tell who is engaged with the work (whether they are speaking or not)? What unspoken rules seem to be in effect? When students watch themselves on videotape, what can we learn from what they say? There is a disciplined emphasis on description, on portraying what is happening, rather than making judgments. This emphasis is enhanced by the use of visual records — videotapes or still photographs — as a tool. It is a difficult discipline for teachers, who usually have well-developed ideas of how classrooms *should* be and often match what they see with an idea already held. Looking with fresh eyes, judgment suspended, can be a new experience.

The Integrative Seminar: Teaching as Collaborative Inquiry (T-322)

The teachers' experience of the program was essentially their experience of this seminar. ("ETP" was often used to refer not to the program but to the seminar.) This is where they came together, throughout the year, to learn from each other and to discuss matters that were important to them. This was the context in which they struggled to become a supportive and productive group. It was from the seminar that this book emerged.

The seminar met on alternate Thursday evenings, for 3 hours, throughout the year. (We found it hard to establish momentum at the beginning, and the following year I made a point of meeting every week for the first 2 months.)

I brought to the seminar the attitudes toward teaching and curriculum briefly outlined above. But I was nervous. My own inclination was always to plan all the readings, the assignments, the activities—even if there was wide scope for different people to go about them in different ways. On the other hand, I had been a party to the powerful experience of previous years, under Catherine Krupnick's direction, when the teachers had given their own design to the seminar sessions. I also knew that teachers had an enormous amount to offer both to each other and to me. In organizing a seminar in my usual way, I would of course have tried to draw on the teachers' experience. But it wouldn't have been the same. I wanted to try my hand at setting up a seminar essentially designed by the teachers.

In my Teaching and Learning course, each reading and assignment was laid out. Perhaps that was why the teachers were willing to accept a seminar in which I did not do that: The other course may have established the belief that I knew very clearly what I was doing and that they could have confidence in the way this was being carried out. (If so, then they had more confidence than I did.)

The name of the seminar, Teaching as Collaborative Inquiry, has remained the same since the program's inception. For me, it had a great deal to do with Claryce Evans's work in teacher-initiated research (Evans, Stubbs, Duckworth, & Davis, 1981). She saw teachers as potential researchers into the nature of teaching in their own classrooms—a great source of understanding about what teaching is (compatible with Donald Schön's (1983) notions of reflective professionals). She set about helping full-time teachers to do that research and to write about it. One element of her work was a biweekly seminar where they could help each other define an area of interest, think about what they already knew about it, and decide what kinds of further information would shed more light on it. Another element was offering each of the teachers in the seminar a graduate student research assistant (in each case, the student was also an experienced teacher) who spent time in the classroom focused on the teacher's issue. Each of these features built collaborative inquiry into the job of teaching. Evans's work was familiar to me by the time we established ETP and significantly influenced my thinking. I sought to incorporate some similar work into the seminar requirements. It took the form of a "fieldwork" requirement that each participant carried out in a local classroom. It is discussed in this book in the February 3 and March 24 sessions.

I made some plans for the very start. I proposed reading Evans and colleagues (1981) and Schön (1983), as well as Bob Davis's book, *What Our High Schools Could Be* (1990). Of the various books written by teachers about their lives and work, this one was current, dealt with public schools, was both passionate and intellectual, and was as honest as any writing about teaching that I knew.

I also knew that I wanted each person to write. I planned to ask for a final paper, but I was also hoping to engage the participants in working on writing about their experience as teachers. I was not sure how this might develop.

Taking my lead from Catherine Krupnick, I decided that each week's seminar would be planned by two of the teachers. I knew from her that this planning needed to be done with great care if a group was to emerge from this collection of people. I counted on being a part of the planning myself — largely to ask questions that the planners might not have thought about, to be sure each detail was considered. (We all felt that my participation became less important as the year went on; nonetheless, plans were always checked with me, in case I could think of an angle or a concern that the two planners had not considered.) Each week's planning meeting included the pair from the previous week to discuss responses to the last session and consider what ideas or feelings needed follow-up.

The planners prepared both the agenda for the evening and the "homework" the participants needed to do ahead of time. As the year went on, we tried to designate each session's leaders well in advance so that they could start their preparing and give people enough time for the assignments. At the start, we only managed to designate the leaders session by session. Given the 2-week interval between sessions, they still were able to give their colleagues a week's notice for the homework assignments. (And in one or two very early cases, as we sought to establish some continuity, the "outgoing" planners proposed some homework that would follow through on the work of the evening.)

Reflective journals, written by each participant, became an important part of the seminar, but they had not been established by me as a requirement. The idea emerged from the group. (See the account of the October 21 session.)

We had at our disposition a file drawer. There we left our journals for everyone in the group to read, and planners left homework assignments and readings for the next session.

Finally, I had learned from Catherine Krupnick in previous years that the first session could become a powerful one by drawing on all of our personal stories, and that this experience could be an important one for creating the joint commitment that the year's work would require.

WRITING THIS BOOK

This book is organized around the sessions of the Integrative Seminar. To reconstruct them, we have drawn on: the planners' written agendas, written homework assignments, transcripts of the few tape-recorded sessions, our memories, and, most important, the reflective journals written after each session by each participant. We have selected journal excerpts partly to present a range of thoughts about the topic, partly to convey something of the quality of the evening, partly to portray the development of the group, and partly to show our different perspectives and feelings—as teachers, as learners, as ordinary human beings.

Inserted among those accounts are some of the teachers' final papers. They are placed as interludes, after sessions whose substance they echo.

We decided late in the year that we might be able to write a book about our experience (see March 24 session). That summer all members of the program agreed to the use of their journals, and a group of us started to meet every 2 weeks (for what turned out to be 2 years!). An individual or a pair took on the writing of a session description and brought a draft to a meeting. It was read by everybody present, and comments were discussed and agreed to jointly. This was done for at least four drafts of each session. Along the way, we discussed and decided questions such as the purpose of the book, how to use the final papers, what kind of introduction was needed, and how to attribute authorship. Before final editing, the manuscript was sent to the absent members, to make sure everything was acceptable to them.

The list of members of the Experienced Teachers Group includes everyone who was in the program. Everyone created the year, and everyone's written work is represented in some way. Chris was our coordinator. In addition to being an active part of the writing team, he kept track of what we needed to get, who was working on what, what we needed to do in any given meeting, which draft of each chapter was the most current, which permission slips needed to be signed by whom. He also took responsibility for the final assembly and formatting of all of the writing. Besides Chris, the members who came to the meetings through the 2 years were Duane, Tracey, Jane, Susan, Kris, and myself. Rosario and Suzy worked with us the first year, while they were still in the area, as did Mark for the first summer. Burry, Doug, Jorge, and Elissa kept in touch from a distance.

The teacher/authors of this book represent elementary, middle, and secondary schools, public and private schools, schools in poor communities and in wealthy ones; we have a few years or decades of experience. The book is an account of our coming to know each other's thinking and practice, and building our own strengths through each other's. We see it as a presentation of teachers' thinking about central current issues and as a potential model for other groups.

Fourteen Teachers

CHRISTOPHER WHITBECK

September 23

We had all read the notice on the door to room 221. "ETP will meet Thursday in Larson G-06 at 6:00 — See you then." A list of names was attached. Ages, backgrounds, and geography were impossible to judge. As we waited in a basement hallway of Larson Hall, all that we knew about each other was that we were teachers, experienced teachers, whatever that meant. There were six men and seven women; short, tall, dressed in everything from ties and skirts to T-shirts. There was some congenial conversation: "Are you here for the ETP program? Hi, my name is. . . . What do you teach? Where? I wonder what we'll do tonight. What T-440 section are you taking?"

At 6:00 Eleanor Duckworth arrived; we followed her into a room that was dimly lit. One wall of windows looked outside to a stairway that led to street level; it was dark, however, and the windows only mirrored reflections of moving bodies and a jumbled assortment of chairs toward the back of the room. We moved two rectangular tables to the side and brought our chairs with their adjustable writing arms into a circle. The small talk continued as the writing arms swung into place. Notebooks came out, and we waited for Eleanor to begin the class. She sat in the circle with her back to the blackboard at the "front" of the room. This would turn out to be the last time that Eleanor was "the teacher." She would soon become a member of the class, not leading or directing in traditional ways, but rather a participant.

After some business about times and schedules, Eleanor suggested that we share what brought each of us to teaching. Her questions were: How did you get into teaching? How does it compare with what you expected? What keeps you there? Three hours later we had not heard from everyone. Fourteen people sat mesmerized listening to stories about growing up and about being teachers. Fourteen strangers began to explore education by exploring their own histories. We began to form a working, collaborative group by sharing and listening to stories about becoming teachers. Our pens were idle, our notebooks blank — we just listened.

To help our readers become more familiar with us, we are including the following biographies written by the teacher or created from each teacher's spoken words. They are an introduction; our personalities, convictions, experiences, questions, and opinions will be revealed as our ETP experience unfolds throughout the rest of the book. For the convenience of the reader who may want to refer back to these biographies, they are presented in alphabetical order by first name.

Teaching was the last job that *Burry Gowen* ever expected to take when he graduated from college. An economics major, Burry went from college directly to banking. After several job changes within the business sector, Burry realized that something was missing and an employment consultant suggested teaching.

Burry had worked as an eighth- and ninth-grade business project volunteer and decided to make the transition to teaching. His first teaching position was in a small town near Seattle. "Every once in a while I get to see the light go on in kids' eyes. . . . I love trying to think of ways to get that light to go on more and more." Burry says that he's never thought twice about being anything else but a teacher.

Always interested in science, *Chris Whitbeck* enrolled in the pre-med program at the State University of New York at Stony Brook. Working on the state hospital's trauma team, he realized that medicine was not what he wanted in life. He transferred into the university's teacher preparation program, and "For the first time in college I did well. I also found the first professor who *cared*. The other professors believed in weeding out rather than teaching."

Chris began teaching in a Boston Spanish bilingual school in 1987 and has taught middle school science in the Brookline Public Schools since 1989. "I feel extremely comfortable in my classroom. I hope that I guide my students as my teaching professor guided me. I hope to help students find the excitement in learning that it took me 20 years to discover."

Doug Jones always knew what he wanted to do for a living. His father, a high school math teacher and administrator, was always able to make Doug understand through a myriad of explanations and examples. Doug attended his father's alma mater, Princeton, where he prepared to teach classical languages and history.

For 11 years Doug has taught math and Latin at an independent school in Cambridge, Massachusetts. While Doug believes that knowledge and enthusiasm for a specific subject can make teaching easier, he is a strong proponent of the view that the best and most efficient learning occurs when students believe that their opinion is valued and that the teacher truly cares about their welfare. Doug seeks to help students learn how to think independently and pursue their interests. "I am excited when my students are eager to probe each issue and question more deeply."

Growing up in California next to his elementary school, *Duane Grobman* viewed school as "my extended backyard. It was a fun place to be — a place to wonder, explore, play, learn." He got to know his teachers well and saw them as unique adults — fascinating and mystical.

In high school he got his first opportunity to teach, teaching 3-year-olds in Sunday School. While in college studying to become an architect, he taught junior high students at the same church. Designing learning experiences increasingly became more interesting than anything he was designing on his drafting board. He left architecture and pursued teaching.

After college Duane served as a church minister of education. Recently he had been teaching first and second grades in a New Mexico public school associated with the Coalition of Essential Schools. Viewing education as "a cultivator of hope," Duane teaches because of a great love for learning and the joy experienced in seeing others learn.

Eleanor Duckworth studied philosophy as an undergraduate. As a graduate student, having been sent with a fellowship to Paris, she happened into a course taught by Jean Piaget, whose ideas have shaped her work ever since.

Later, as a Ph.D. dropout, she found that her work with Piaget was of interest to elementary school science curriculum designers, who hired her despite her limited knowledge of either education or science. The Elementary Science Study proved to be a remarkable educational grounding, and she has been involved in teacher education ever since.

Eleanor is currently professor of education at Harvard University. During this work, she was chair of the Teaching, Curriculum and Learning Environments department.

Elissa Wolf became interested in teaching as a volunteer tutor of junior high students in Middletown, Connecticut, while attending Wesleyan University. Initially, she turned down teaching offers; but living in Boston for several months with no employment, Elissa was tempted into accepting a co-teaching position in a K-3 after-school program. She thrived on the energy of the children but realized that she wanted both to teach history and to work with older students.

She was offered a teaching internship at an independent school in Colorado and became a passionate teacher and coach. "I am rewarded by the undescribable effect of seeing a kid 'get it' after months of struggle. I feel very fortunate to have stumbled upon a profession in which I feel the importance of what we do on a daily basis."

Jane Kays always wanted to become a nurse, but this was also a time when family decisions were made by the head of the household. In Jane's case, her mother said, "Be a teacher." Jane complied.

Jane grew up in Chelsea, Massachusetts. Her friends and classmates were Gypsies, blacks, Poles, and the few remaining Jewish children who were all living in a neighborhood that was rapidly declining as a result of the many fires that ravaged the city. These developmental years influenced Jane's decision, upon starting her first teaching job 25 years ago, to teach in disadvantaged neighborhoods. "I knew I wanted to teach children who resembled those with whom I had been educated. . . . The inner city seemed to be a place where I could make a significant contribution." Jane has always taught elementary grades in the Boston public schools.

Jorge Mejia studied engineering for 2 years following high school in his native Colombia. Leaving engineering, he chose to study education at McGill University before entering a seminary to become a priest. After 6 months, Jorge decided to leave the seminary.

He returned to teach in the Colombian school where he grew up. Jorge has also been a social worker but knew that his 2 years teaching had been the happiest years of his life. "I decided then that's what I was going to do for the rest of my life, and my decision has been confirmed through the last 5 years of teaching."

Kris Newton teaches physics at Cambridge Rindge and Latin School, the public high school in Cambridge, Massachusetts. While pursuing a degree in mechanical engineering at the Massachusetts Institute of Technology, Kris became interested in teaching and also enrolled in an undergraduate teacher education program at Wellesley College.

"I enjoy teaching physics for many reasons, but partly because there's so much more to learn. I'd never been in a job where I started to become more curious or wonder about things. I've also had something to do with helping my students see and wonder about the world in a similar way and that was neat.

"I also love my school. The staff is supportive and the school is the most diverse community I have ever been in. So that's what keeps me in teaching: the school, the kids, and learning about science."

From his elementary school principal, to a graduate student who convinced him to return to high school after he had quit, teachers have helped

Mark Schoeffel realize that there were amazing things to know if he spent time trying to discover and share them.

Mark's best experiences at schools were in communities and in conversations where he could feel a part of something special. It was those experiences that he wanted to re-create when he began teaching at the independent high school he had attended in Toronto. "I really wanted to be like some of the people that I respected and admired who were just passionate about teaching; I didn't want to do anything else. I don't do it with a kind of zealotry . . . I do it with a spirit of laughter and an undercurrent of seriousness. I love it." Making personal differences in students' lives keeps Mark teaching.

As an undergraduate in Colombia, *Rosario Jaramillo* loved history, but that was not an academic option in the country at that time. She majored in political science and then started teaching history in Bogotá. She discovered that teaching and learning were far more difficult than she had anticipated. After getting married and having two daughters, she went to the United States and studied political science and educational policy.

Returning to Colombia, she coordinated a team that created a new social studies curriculum. She wasn't too sure that writing a curriculum outside the classroom was a very good idea, so after 6 years at the Ministry she went into the classroom again.

"At our school in Bogotá [run by the American Franciscan Sisters], we tried to teach a consciousness of how it is to live in a country like ours, how to make decisions that are important for one's personal life and for others, and how to work hard to change the situations we can really affect, without worrying too much about the failure of the big revolutions."

Finally, there was a degree program in history she was able to enter in Colombia. Immediately after handing in her master's thesis, she came to Harvard to prepare herself to reenter the classroom with a fresh outlook on teaching history.

Susan McCray was influenced by her mother, the principal of a Quaker school in New York City, and her grandfather, who reminded her that *rabbi* means "teacher" and that a rabbi is the most revered member of a Jewish community.

Struggling as a student who received remedial help in elementary school, Susan grew up believing that there were secrets to writing known to everyone but her. "I can still see the red marks covering my papers."

Her first "teaching" experience as an instructor at the North Carolina Outward Bound School taught her to challenge people beyond their preconceived limits. She also taught at an alternative public school in Dorchester,

Massachusetts. At the South Bronx High School/New York Outward Bound Center, she integrated the philosophy and methodology of experiential learning into classroom academic instruction "Education is a form of political action; besides, young people have so much to give; this makes me want to give in return."

Suzy Ort was inspired to become a teacher by another teacher. In a college class with Dr. Theodore Sizer, "I started to challenge my assumptions about what constitutes school practice. Taking a historical look at schooling in the United States helped me to begin formulating a new vision." After graduation, Suzy applied for "emergency certification" as a social studies teacher in the New York City public school system. Interested in working with students who had been discouraged by their previous school experiences, she began teaching at University Heights High School, an alternative school in the Bronx affiliated with the Coalition of Essential Schools. Her motivation to teach stems from a commitment to public institutions: "Public schools are one of the few remaining spaces where people gather in pursuit of a larger democratic ideal."

Tracey Guth became interested in schools as a freshman in college when she volunteered in a Boston high school. This experience led her to apply to the Undergraduate Teacher Education Program at Harvard. She even student-taught but did not yet realize that teaching was her calling. However, she liked it enough to move to Manhattan and fight the city's extraordinary bureaucracy in search of a job. She was hired to teach social studies at a large public high school in Brooklyn.

In the middle of her first year, she was told that because of budget cuts she would lose her job in January. Tracey realized, "I don't want to be fired because I really like this." She had finally made the decision that teaching was what she wanted to do. Ultimately, Tracey was not let go and taught there for 3 years.

We learned a lot about each other that evening, but that was just the beginning. Our voices are heard through the journal entries selected for the session descriptions that follow.

"Fasten Your Seatbelts. . . . It's Going to Be a Bumpy Ride"

DUANE GROBMAN II

October 7

Our first session had been an evening of listening and laughing together, of eating Eleanor's home-grown grapes and hearing from others the joys and trials of teaching. I remember being put in a near-trance by each story—so rich, so diverse, and yet in wonderful and meaningful ways connecting to the experiences of others in the group. In the weeks that followed, I both reflected on individuals' stories and looked with anticipation to hearing more from our group members.

Eleanor had explained in the first session that this course was student-run, and thus pairs of us would facilitate each session. She explained that after each class she and Rosario would meet with the facilitators from the past session and the upcoming session for both debriefing and planning. She then asked for two volunteers to meet with her to plan our next session. Burry and I naively raised our hands.

If I had been disciplined then (as I would become later) to write a journal of my thoughts of each class session, my journal for that first week would have concluded something like this:

> What possessed me to raise my hand? I'm usually not the type to vol-
> unteer for something before I really know what it is I'm volunteering
> for. Our brave Burry was the first to raise his hand after Eleanor solic-
> ited two volunteers to plan our second session. Then there was that
> moment of silence and staring at the floor, followed by my temporary
> lapse of sanity. What possessed me to raise my hand? I know I volun-
> teered to help in the planning, but it still isn't clear to me what this
> class, this year-long group learning experience, is all about. We don't
> even have a syllabus or course outline to guide us. All we have is our
> experience as teachers and our ongoing questions. Thinking back to
> our first session, I realize that is, in fact, a considerable mountain to

mine. But where do we begin? In which direction do we go? What do we look at first? Where do we start our "collaborative inquiry"? And what is "collaborative inquiry" anyway? If this is going to be an expedition in constructivist learning, I'd best confess at our planning meeting that I hold a teacher's credential not a contractor's license. What did possess me to raise my hand?

Our meeting was on a Friday morning in the cafeteria. The four of us got hot drinks and bagels and then got down to business. It soon became apparent that I was not alone in my perplexity and pondering about our planning. Burry and Rosario also came with similar feelings and questioning. Eleanor relied on our questions to guide us. Questions such as:

What do we do?

What do you want to do?

What have groups done in the past?

Looked at understanding diversity, gender inequalities, discussed Kozol's Savage Inequalities *[1991]. But don't let that dictate your thinking and planning.*

Do we really not have a syllabus or guiding plan?

I have some ideas to start you off, but your experiences as teachers will be your guiding plan.

We met for approximately 2 hours, and then Burry and I were left to discuss planning on our own. Eleanor gave two suggestions for readings to get us started: a chapter from *The Reflective Practitioner*, by Donald Schön (1983), and a report entitled, "Teacher-Initiated Research," by Claryce Evans and colleagues (1981). These were resources that looked good, partly because of the ideas each set forth but also because they gave Burry and me some direction after the extreme openness with which Eleanor positioned our planning.

Burry suggested we look at the course description in the catalogue. This might have been a piece of information individuals in the group used in making their decision to apply to the Experienced Teachers Program. The description read:

T-322   TEACHING AS COLLABORATIVE INQUIRY

This course is required of and limited to students in the Experienced Teachers Program. It considers theories and collaborative strategies for inquiring into and improving school practice. The focus is on practice-based questions and the use of a variety of kinds of information that bear on these questions: for example, case studies, classroom observation, journals, clinical interviewing, video records, autobiography. Students will spend time in a school site. Readings will deal with relationships between theory and practice, and with specific issues that arise in the course of the year.

The two of us wondered how individuals understood this description. What if we printed it out and took time to discuss it in class? We were struck by the mentioning of "theories" and "practice" as well as the emphasis on inquiry and "practice-based questions." We were interested in learning what sense others made of these words as well as the collection of words this description included. We decided it should be part of our evening.

We met on our own for several hours; we talked on the phone over the weekend; and then we met a second time with Eleanor and Rosario to go over plans. It took hours, again, for their feedback and suggestions. (Frightened future facilitators were appalled and awed that it took 7 to 10 hours to plan a session.) The four of us finally decided on the following plan:

6:00 Continue personal stories (Rosario, Doug, Eleanor)

6:35 Read course description and discuss. This would be an introduction to the homework assignment (See Figure 1).

6:50 Small-group discussion: What unsolved problems/questions do you have in your teaching? Share your reflections about them, that is, given Schön's ideas about reflecting, and with the help of others in your group, get outside of yourself and look at your problem/question.

7:20 Break

7:35 Discussion of readings

8:05 "Success Stories"—Share a success story from your teaching experience

8:20 Group building and debriefing: Share something that came out of our discussion this evening, from another, that you thought was meaningful. Why was it meaningful to you?

8:40 "Housekeeping" (Our administrative checklist)
  1. Sign up for bringing snacks
  2. Fieldwork placement ideas
  3. Facilitators for next class
  4. Homework assignment

9:00 Conclude

These were our plans for the evening. We would learn in this session, as well as in many of the sessions that followed, that our plans didn't always match the experience of the evening. As experienced teachers, this wasn't a

FIGURE 1. Reading Discussion Questions, October 7

I. *Teacher Initiated Research* (Evans et al., 1981)

1. Do you agree or disagree with the author's opening statement? Why or why not? (p. 8)
2. How do you react/respond to the author's claim that: "They don't talk seriously to each other *and so* they don't take themselves seriously as a group. They don't talk seriously to each other *because* they don't take themselves seriously as a group"? (p. 8)
3. Evans writes: "The schools failed to provide an environment which was professional and supportive for teachers as much as they failed to teach students" (p. 3). How would you describe the professional environment in which you taught? What was most missing for you?
4. Evans criticizes existing staff development, including in-services (p. 5). What has been your experience and your assessment of it?
5. What question of your own did this article prompt?

II. *The Reflective Practitioner* (Schön, 1983)

1. Schön writes: "Professionals themselves have shown signs recently of a loss of confidence in their claims to extraordinary knowledge" (p. 5).
   • Do you agree this is true for the teaching profession?
   • How do you assess your own confidence level?
2. "Professionals are called upon to perform the tasks for which they have not been educated" (pp. 14–15).
   • How do you feel about your own teaching preparation/training?
   • How would you have liked it to have been better/more effective?
3. Share a time teaching in which you experienced "reflecting-in-action" or, as the baseball player phrases it, "finding the groove."
4. What is your evaluation/assessment of your own "reflecting-in-action"?
5. Do you agree with Tolstoy's statement, "Good teaching requires not a method but an art"? How would you describe/articulate that art?

Homework assignment due Wednesday, October 13. Please complete and put in Herbert (Burry) Gowen's mailbox no later than 6:30 PM. This is so that it can be used in the planning of the October 21 session.

   Now that we have begun the process of clarifying our strengths and quantifying areas that we would like to address in this seminar, we would like you to fill out this questionnaire. In so doing, please be specific, if specifics are appropriate to your situation. By collating these questionnaires next week, we hope to develop a short list of topics and issues that must be addressed in order for the participants to feel fulfilled by their participation in this seminar.

1. What would you like to experience through this seminar (expectations, topics covered, experiences desired)? Feel free to use more paper. Feel free to make lists.
2. What would you not like not to have done through this seminar? (The *one thing* that if at the end of the year we have not done you will feel ripped off)

new revelation. Nonetheless, we planned enough for two sessions—our schedule wasn't realistic. It became a reminder to facilitators to be flexible and to expect the unexpected (which wasn't always possible).

Our discussion of the course description was lively and lengthy, derailing our time schedule while we searched for a definition of "collaborative inquiry." We briefly looked at the homework sheet for our next class. One question was particularly thought-provoking: "What would you not like not to have done through this seminar?" (Yes, we were aware of the double negative.)

The small-group discussions about unsolved problems and issues in our lives as teachers elicited a wide variety of responses. A sampling of those shared include: the isolated nature of teaching, "territorialist teachers" and working as a team, assessment, "curriculum that enhances student understanding," pedagogy that improves student learning, student motivation, teacher evaluation as a support mechanism, faculty morale, national and local school reform movements, moral development and character education, and managing the various roles in which teachers find themselves.

We had hoped that our questions on the readings would give the group a way to start talking about their work as teachers, but the discussion of the readings brought mixed reviews, with some members being engaged by the readings while others were not. My recollection is that some members felt it was too early to jump into a discussion on reflecting. Did we know each other well enough after one week to do that? This reluctance was also brought to light during our abbreviated discussion of "success stories." There was strong consensus among the group that they did not want to share "success stories." Hence we did not. However, several of us talked in the weeks that followed of the dilemma many teachers face. Thinking of the schools in which we taught, if we shared our "success stories" with other teachers we feared being perceived as boastful, proud, arrogant, or prescriptive, all of which the culture of teaching (and perhaps our personal convictions) told us to avoid. Yet we realized that here, at a school of education, if no one shared their successes, or, to put it another way, "what worked for me," how would we learn from one another? It was a dilemma we faced but were just beginning to talk about.

This was one dilemma. Another was that we were "experienced teachers" facilitating a class, not knowing what it was supposed to look like and at the same time wanting to be as inclusive of everyone's perspective as possible. These dilemmas left Burry and me, the two in the driver's seat for the evening, to do much reflecting. If I had known then what I know now, I would have shared with Jane and Jorge (our facilitators for the following session) a variant of that famous Bette Davis movie quote: "Fasten your seatbelts. It's going to be a bumpy ride."

For our first month I think most of us viewed our year of learning together through eyes of ignorance and idealism, eyes that perceived the road ahead as smooth, level, with wonderful sites to explore along the way. Our year together would reveal that the ride was bumpy; for a variety of reasons we didn't have seatbelts, and our thoughts and feelings about teaching, and each other, were frequently jostled about as we journeyed through "Teaching as Collaborative Inquiry" together.

Let's Make a Deal

JANE KAYS

October 21

Jorge: As a facilitator, I must say that though it wasn't a teacher-centered session, I felt completely exhausted after finishing. It's difficult to realize how much energy is spent until you finish. I have to admit that I felt frustrated when the class was over, but I didn't know the reason at the time. Now I realize that I had an unconscious objective: to have a curriculum established by 9:00. Why? There's nothing wrong with postponing objectives or even changing them. I learned a lot about building curriculum. One of the questions that comes to mind is how much of it can be imposed and how much is self-defined. I visualize a spectrum that goes from a completely self-defined (what we tried to do) to a completely imposed curriculum (what usually happens). The ideal would be somewhere in between, depending on the teacher and the students.

Jane: As we entered the final segment of the class and attempted to mesh our plans into a "communal vision," I had fewer favorable feelings about our format. I left feeling frustrated that we did not leave with a year's plan; I felt confused about how a democratically run session finds consensus without belaboring the point; I shared Kris's concern that we had not done enough, and, as the facilitator, I felt responsible.

Session 3 brought together Jorge, a math teacher from Bogotá, and myself, an elementary school teacher from the Boston public schools. We volunteered to lead this session because we felt a need to confront this unknown, and perhaps daunting, leadership task with the immediacy of one who charters an unknown, yet exciting, "course." We did not share an interest in a specific topic that we wished to develop for our colleagues, but rather a sense of "let's do it!" There had seemed to be an uncomfortable lull thus far, and Jorge and I were eager to move the group forward under the guise of any of the suggested topic requests gathered from our colleagues.

From the previous session we inherited an assortment of course expectations. The topics that the group indicated in their homework were varied. They targeted traditional themes such as motivation and assessment as well as current notions that applied to school reform issues and community learning. We hoped to design our session around these responses and culminate the evening with a flexible agenda for the year.

After many meetings and many false starts, Jorge suggested we use curriculum as our topic. How obvious it then seemed. If we intended to create our own agenda for the year, were we not developing our own curriculum? We would begin the class with a brief discussion about curriculum — its meaning and/or connotations. Next, three groups would work independently for an hour to design a curriculum for the seminar. Prepared to record their ideas on blank chart paper, each group would use the homework responses to carve a path for the seminar to follow throughout the year. We would then come together, display and explain each group's respective plan, and determine which plan or plans we would like to use.

Our vision seemed uncomplicated, but, by the end of the session, too little time, too much to do, and so many different opinions set the frustrating tone that is embedded in our reflections. What had seemed to be a simple assignment became complex when we realized that each chart should be reviewed and discussed (see Figure 2). Some groups even became persuasive, as though we were an audience who needed some convincing about which plan to adopt.

> *Elissa:* I have mixed feelings about Thursday's class. I left the room feeling both a sense of accomplishment and frustrated. I thought the facilitators' plan was a good one, and it allowed for some intense small-group work — something I think is effective and that I enjoy. The idea of coming together as a whole group for the final hour also made sense. In the end, it seemed as if we had an important and exciting task on our hands with too little time to completely confront it.

> *Kris:* I don't know where to begin. I was apprehensive about last week's class meeting. Maybe *apprehensive* is too strong a word. I was very eager to get settled down on what we were going to do for the year. I don't feel as though the course has started yet, and I would like it to. . . . The class started off slowly. When we broke into groups I was thinking, "Not this again. Are we going to break into groups every time?" . . . Our group had a hard time getting going. We were unsure of our mission and unsure where to begin. We fumbled around for 10–15 minutes before inspiration began to flow. Then we decided to come up with one or more overall themes and fit topics into that

framework. Susan suggested the bowl theme, and we went with it. We began filling in the curriculum and also coming up with methods for use in each class meeting. . . . I was beginning to feel very invested in our class. . . . Eventually we went back to the large group. I was very anxious to begin to talk as a large group and come to a consensus about some of our ideas. I was actually rushing people to finish with the break. We then spent time looking over every group's charts. I was worried that we were wasting time, and I was getting frustrated. I was starting to worry that we would not come to an agreement by the end of the class, and I did not want to leave again feeling like we didn't have a plan.

Doug: At times I found last night's class to be extremely rewarding and fulfilling, while at other times I was frustrated and exasperated. It was a huge relief to be chatting with my experienced colleagues once again and escape from the overwhelming idealism of the nonexperienced teachers in other classes.

I enjoyed having a chance to begin to discuss actual themes and goals of our class for this year; however, I became extremely eager to actually discuss these ideas — not to talk about how or when we are going to talk about them.

Susan: It was frustrating, tiring, exciting, infuriating, overwhelming, exhilarating; we were students. And that is how students should feel. Think about the expansiveness of the questions we faced. What are we doing here, and how are we going to do whatever we are doing here? Feel the anxiety that that blank page evoked. Think about how engaged we were in the process of filling that page. Imagine our students who engaged in their learning. If you are part of defining a mission or vision, then you are invested in the struggle of achieving it.

Suzy: I love discussion classes. I love organized focused discussions that go off on rich tangents. I love reading groups. I love (this might be called "like") to think about "group" and to participate in building a trusting and fulfilling one. Our ETP class has the potential to be all these things, and I am psyched about it. Last Thursday's class showed how hard it can be, though. I think we got a little daunted at the beginning with the pressure of planning a curriculum. Perhaps we might have begun with the thought of planning for the year, creating a plan rather than a curriculum. For me at least, the word *curriculum* brings flashes of commitment, inflexibility, and the Bored of Education. I

FIGURE 2. **Three Curriculum Models**

Model one
1. Teacher collaboration
2. Assessment
3. Instructional techniques/interdisciplinary teaching
4. Tension between "freedom and direction"
5. Motivational strategies (student and teacher)
6. Questioning, probing, inquiry, discussion (understanding students'
        understanding)
7. Heterogeneous groups
8. Managing teacher roles (school-based management)
9. Writing (reflective practitioner)
10. Classroom management/discipline
11. School reform and Coalition Schools
12. Reality to fantasy

Model two

Pedagogy

This Class   **Fieldwork**   **Future experience**

Experience

Strategies

Heterogeneous groups	Collaboration
Cooperative learning	Discussions
Writing	Student-centered
Freedom vs. direction	Understanding

Assessment	**Questions**	**Teacher Roles**
Documentation		Researcher
Teacher and student reflection		Coach
Understanding		Involvement with students
		Manager

Schools	**Atmosphere**
Coalition	Motivation
Inner-city youth	Risk taking
Staff relations	Multiculturalism
Social responsibility	Safe/no violence
Historical context	
Parents	

Fieldwork

How does it relate to individual questions?

Model three: "The Bowls" Curriculum

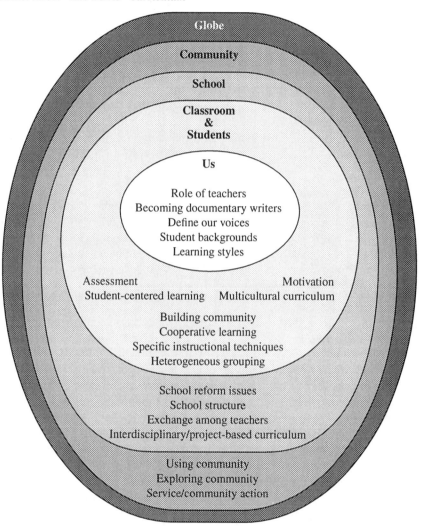

Globe

Community

School

Classroom
&
Students

Us

Role of teachers
Becoming documentary writers
Define our voices
Student backgrounds
Learning styles

Assessment   Motivation
Student-centered learning   Multicultural curriculum

Building community
Cooperative learning
Specific instructional techniques
Heterogeneous grouping

School reform issues
School structure
Exchange among teachers
Interdisciplinary/project-based curriculum

Using community
Exploring community
Service/community action

Facilitator Responsibilities:
1. Follow overall flow
2. Adapt to group's needs
3. Build from previous session
    to move us forward as a group
4. Model strategies
5. Integrate readings and theory
6. Guide reflection/debrief/evaluate

Strategies and Experiences:
1. Chronicle ourselves via writing and
    responding weekly
2. Journal
3. Weave personal experiences throughout
4. Reading and discussion
5. Modeling your approach

say this, yet my small group seemed undaunted by the task. *Au contraire*. It was very productive, interesting, elucidatory, and fun.

If the process of collaborative inquiry is to be embraced, then fundamental to that idea is collaboration in curriculum development. We sought to develop a communal vision around the year's curriculum. However, in words like *communal* and *collaborative* there are undertones of partnerships and togetherness. There is the suggestion that the parties to the process are, in some way, involved with each other. After only three sessions together, our group seemed eager to become a community, but we were a group in name only. The following reflections explore some aspects of our frustration.

Mark: I feel a bit overwhelmed with what happened in the last 2 hours of the ETP class on Thursday, October 21, 1993. After all, I had felt that as a group, we were all excited to be together, to talk about teaching, to listen and learn from one another's experience. It was not clear to me what people were frustrated with—some seemed frustrated with the fact that other people were not frustrated enough.

Duane: When we regrouped after the break and put up our poster on the board, I sensed a change of climate in the air. Sarcastic comments began to blow, and I was not surprised to see what followed. Although we had a very brief glance at the other posters, our understanding of each other's labor and thought was grossly limited. Hence, certain individuals in the group pushed their thoughts (described on the poster) as if they were a salesperson. At the end of the session I felt pressure to buy one of the three products and go with it. My sought-after decision was reduced to a choice between the "bowl proposal," the "graph proposal," or the "list proposal." With 9:00 P.M. arriving I sensed some feeling of the need to "make a deal" so that we would know what's ahead. I, for one, even if we did "make a deal," was not sure what the deal entailed (let alone looked like).

Chris: Gathering together as a large group, was it impractical to believe that we would set a curriculum for the course in 1 hour? Was this what anyone believed would happen? Would or should we please everyone? I believed the pedagogy should be set. So there was at least one person who believed this. I think that others wanted this to happen. Would we please everyone? I don't believe this is possible, although I remain hopeful.

Suzy: Working collaboratively is very difficult. It takes a long time. It takes a lot longer than if one person were to stand up in front of us and tell us what we will do. Getting used to giving yourself and your group enough time to figure it out is challenging. Knowing when or if "enough time" has been spent is even more challenging.

As teachers we are all too familiar with lessons that (seem to) require neat endings. Bells remind us that it is time to move on to another group or topic. With each Pavlovian ring we dutifully attempt to wrap up our lessons. How do we create a sense of continuity in the classroom, when we are pressed into a stop/start mode? If there is no end in our learning, then there are no new beginnings — only continuations and bridges as we advance from different points of understanding. This class ended in haste, leaving many of us with questions about our need for neater endings.

Tracey: So what do I think we should do about T-322?. . . . I kept vacillating back and forth between wanting a specific plan and wanting to take things as they come. The need some of us have for a specific plan of action reflects our schools and teaching — we are very goal-oriented. I would be comfortable with choosing a general plan, outlining a few main topics we wish to cover in order. But we should not have a topic for each week — I think we need to intentionally leave space to get "bogged" down in the valleys. That is, after all, a reason I took a year off to sink myself deeply into debt here at HGSE. I am pleased that we decided to write these reflections and to comment on each other's. We also basically agreed that, whatever the topic, those leading the session would try to model a teaching strategy. Slow going as it is, our curriculum is making progress.

Suzy: How can we avoid the last-minute rushed decision because we have run out of time and we need to make a decision before class runs out or else? Or else what? Nothing really, but we are, I am, used to thinking this way. Resolution. Finished. Packaged. Done. Crossed off my list.

Mark: Why did I want everything to be all hunky-dory, straight-line, agreed-upon, consensus-based, in so quick a time? Why are we teachers so impatient with ourselves and with each other, and even impatient about another's impatience, that we lose sight of the long-term goal of learning in favor of a short-term goal of consensus and/or "clear" purpose?

At 9:00 few felt finished, and to most members, it mattered. As

Suzy acknowledged her race with the clock, she also questioned the pace. Let the clock run out. Let's think about process and content. While each small group worked to develop a common vision for the course, all worked diligently. However, [when we came together,] anxiety replaced diligence and frustration shadowed our accomplishments.

At the end of class Jorge, Eleanor, and I asked everyone to think and write about what had become apparent about curriculum development. The group agreed and began writing biweekly about something they (we) noticed, wondered about, learned, got upset about — these were starters to be used or not. This suggestion/assignment was the beginning of the reflections that became a critical part of the seminar.

Two copies of the reflections were due in "the drawer" on the Wednesday following each session. One copy stayed in the drawer and was available to everyone for perusal; a designated person took the second copy each week to read, respond to, and return to the author at the next class. These reflections are, in fact, the heart of this book. They are our conversations with each other as well as with ourselves. In the reflections many of us searched for answers to, perhaps, unanswerable questions. They reveal our insights and our inquiries.

Rome Fell, and Nothing Much Happened for a While

CHRISTOPHER WHITBECK

November 4

Confusion, frustration, and a feeling of discomfort pervaded last week's meeting. Mark, Jane, Jorge, Eleanor, and I met to analyze what had happened in the class and what needed to happen next.

It became evident to us that the group was unhappy with two things. First, we had set an unrealistic goal, expecting to choose one complete outline. Second, we were planning and planning; but when were we going to begin? The seminar was not moving forward. We didn't feel as if we were learning.

In our planning meeting Mark, Eleanor, and I decided that it was important to start by *doing* something. Further curriculum planning, which we knew needed to be done, would be left until the latter half of the evening (see Figure 3).

So the evening began with a discussion of curriculum as teachers encounter it, live with it, embrace or create it. Impetus for discussion came from Bob Davis (1990), and many of us, like Jorge, shared our experiences and dreams of what schools could be.

Jorge: Last class was very didactic because I came with the perspective of someone who knew very little about the subject of curricula. I have to confess that the idea of not having a curriculum hadn't crossed my mind before coming to Harvard. In our first meeting, when some people said that they were given a piece of chalk and nothing else at the beginning of the year, I was shocked. "How could that be?" I thought. To give you an idea of what went through my mind, let me tell you what I used to do. For the year's program, I used to copy the table of contents from the textbook. I didn't do it out of laziness, nor was it imposed. I could have done other things that would have been accepted by school administrators. I simply didn't know better.

FIGURE 3. Homework Assignment, November 4

I. In the first half of class we will be asking some of you to talk about your own experiences with a set curriculum that you had to follow. We will be interested in hearing from both people who worked within a curriculum they liked and those who worked within a curriculum they disliked. We will also be asking some of you to share your experiences creating an alternative curriculum.

The following quotes from Davis (1990) are included to stimulate your thoughts on curriculum:

      1. Working within a set curriculum—pp. 43–44
      2. Working with a curriculum he disliked—pp. 175–176
      3. Creating curriculum—pp. 16–17

Questions on Davis to stimulate thinking and discussion about curriculum:

1. Davis argues that curriculum development is the best answer to student apathy and streaming. How does he suggest that a curriculum might do this?
   a. What are some of the weaknesses to his argument?
   b. What are some of the strengths?
   c. Is this approach possible where you work?
2. Davis applies much of the responsibility for regulating the teaching of ideas, points of view, passing on beliefs, etc. to a greater authority than teachers.
   a. Who do you think this greater authority might be?
   b. What do you think the role of the teacher needs to be in addressing ideology with which they do not agree?
3. Davis creates a new curriculum to preserve "passing on a legacy, liberal ideas of individual and minority liberties, and the radical challenge of equality and the building of a new society" (p. 17).
   a. What are your goals in creating a new curriculum?
   b. How much may a curriculum represent the points of view of the curriculum designers?

II. The second half of the class will address the issue of our seminar's curriculum. Please observe what we (Chris and Mark) and all class participants do during the first section of class. Be aware of how our structure of the first part of class corresponds to or differs from what you want out of this course and our discussion last week. Our goal in the second part of class will be to develop a working list of objectives for the class. This list will be based on this week's experiences as well as outlines made by each group during last week's class.

So now I'm trying to assimilate as much information as I can. I know that a rigid curriculum is flawed, but the other extreme is not the solution either. We have seen this in our own attempts to create curriculum for this class.

I liked Rosario's defense of curriculums. If we see them as guides and as sources of ideas, they are very helpful. Here is where I add my own ideas. I will play the devil's advocate. In a "curriculumless" school, we have to assume autonomous students and teachers. I have seen too many mediocre teachers to not be afraid of a lack of a guide, and I'll accept it, a control. From this perspective, I see the curriculum as a protection for the children. The type of education that Hawkins (1974) [a reading for T-440] envisions requires a commitment not all teachers are willing or able to make. Why do I say "able"? Not because they are stupid, but because they literally don't have the time.

The struggle between depth and breadth, especially when imposed from outside, quickly became a focus, and Tracey shared her approach to teaching the history of Western Europe: "Rome fell, and nothing much happened for a while. Men rode around on horses and people were very religious." Such summation is obviously not the ideal way to teach students about the Middle Ages. However, Tracey taught in Brooklyn, New York, and therefore was constrained by a state curriculum as well as her school's practice of addressing that curriculum — devoting one semester (half a year) to teaching all of Western European history from the classical Greeks through World War I.

As crammed as such a semester might seem, Western Europe was actually allotted significantly more time than other non-American regions. For example, the history and culture of Africa, the Middle East, and Latin America were all included in a single semester. The students in Tracey's school, 100% nonwhite, were conscious of this disparity, and Tracey decided to address the situation by spending 7 or 8 days studying Columbus's voyages to the Americas and their impact on different regions of the world. (This course of study occurred in the fall of 1992, and the constant stream of articles and news stories surrounding the five-hundredth anniversary of the first voyage provided the initial inspiration — as well as lots of reading material.) However, in order to spend that much time (a significant percentage of the days in the semester), something else had to go, and, thus, "Rome fell."

As Tracey related her story during our discussion, the group latched onto the phrase "Rome fell, and nothing much happened for a while." It expressed not only members' individual past experiences with curricula but also the group's present difficulties. Clearly, ETP was not going to be able to discuss all of the interesting topics suggested by each member. The issues of what to discuss, how deep to go, and, most important, never seeming to really finish anything, were recurrent. Group members could often be heard exclaiming "Rome fell . . . " ETP, fortunately, did not fall, but instead rose to the challenge, made decisions, and moved forward with a flexible framework that we agreed could not include all of our questions and ideas about teaching but needed to evolve continually based on the needs of the group.

> *Tracey:* Everyone worked hard to focus on how our curriculum could work. . . . Mark and Chris deserve high marks for taking the frustration we all felt at the previous session and turning those feelings into something positive. I think that the general discussion on curricula that we had for the first part of class was not only interesting, it is a discussion that I think was a direct response to the events (and frustrations) of the previous week. This is why I, personally, want us to have enough flexibility in our curriculum — so we can fully respond to issues that arise.

We managed, this time, to integrate all three plans to the satisfaction of every one of us. The flexibility that Tracey sought was found in what became known as the "bowl" framework (see Figure 2). The "bowls" provided discussion topics, illustrated possible relationships among topics, provided facilitator responsibilities, and suggested other features to incorporate into the seminar. There was no strict order for the topics. Different individuals indicated topics they wanted to discuss. The group committed itself to those as a minimum.

> *Elissa:* I liked what we ended up with — essentially all the models into one framework. Pretty amazing if you think about it. Fourteen people agreeing on a framework for a course that might actually meet everyone's needs. I am looking forward to this. I also am excited to head into some of the "topics" people highlighted as important for them to consider.

There was a sense of accomplishment, and we also realized that this process, the time that it took, and the many discussions that led to our decision were an integral part of creating a working curriculum. The time that we had spent had not been an abstract exercise. We had experienced firsthand what it meant to create curriculum. The many discussions, the passion, the hard work helped us understand how important curriculum is to a course. We saw the significance that student input can have toward making a curriculum meaningful.

> *Doug:* I was glad that Mark and Chris were willing to be bold and decide the path of the class in a definitive and almost tyrannical way, since this forced us to accept their path or demand an alternative. I have no idea if this was their purpose, but it certainly was effective. . . .
>
> I have to agree with Duane that I was not able to appreciate the structure of the other models until I had had a chance to reflect on just what they were proposing; furthermore, I would have to concur that they all said the same thing in different ways. This realization made me wonder how different our "set" curricula are from our ideal curricula. Could they merely be worded in a way we don't understand or appreciate? Every time we complain about a curriculum, perhaps we should be forced to create our own and compare the two. Perhaps we would discover how little difference there would be. In addition, maybe the exhaustive and impossible curriculum set for some courses is one way of forcing us to make personal decisions as to what we should cover quickly and what we should take some time on.
>
> It would be a nice luxury to have students actually guide us in the creation of the curriculum.

It was important for each of us to express our opinions. In so doing, we were beginning to take responsibility for running the seminar. Facilitators planned and outlined formats for the evening, but more than one person noted that each member had input toward what actually happened each evening. When Tracey taught, she had the flexibility to say, "Rome fell, and then nothing much happened for a while." Class members also realized that they had the right to demand such flexibility within the seminar. Some felt comfortable with the degree to which we were doing this, and some felt we still had a distance to go. If we were still uncomfortable expressing our needs, imagine the difficulty our students would have expressing theirs.

> *Doug:* I was pleased that the group felt comfortable expressing their preferences. Specifically, the freedom that Rosario felt to request that we not break up into small groups showed a huge step in our path toward openness and acceptance of each other's thoughts.

> *Duane:* I thought it was interesting that the class on two occasions during the course of the evening made the decision to stay together as a large group and not break down into small groups. . . . I personally feel the need to hear from all at this point in the course. I greatly value

what each person brings to the class as well as the revelations they may receive while being there.

Chris: I was fascinated with the flexibility and fluidity with which we moved from one idea to the next. The atmosphere within the seminar was one of extreme interest in what each other had to say. It was also a safe atmosphere. People listened and thought about ideas before responding. . . . The importance of a safe, sharing environment in which to study applies as much here as it does in our own classrooms.

Jane: The kind of dialogue we experienced last Thursday is what I hoped ETP would bring. I want to discuss educational issues in depth from many different perspectives. The diversity of our group has the potential for offering varied viewpoints that will reveal more than one face of an issue.

But there was something missing. I cannot put my finger on it, so I'll throw out a few wild guesses. It felt like we were all behaving — not that we hadn't "behaved" before, but that we wanted the session to be a good one. It felt very neat. We wanted to follow the rules. That's an interesting point, because we are trying to be about "loose rules"! If we all had been "looser," we might have gone off on a tangent — will that be allowed? What if when Doug told us how he designs his Latin curriculum around what he knows best, we debated whether all teachers should only teach what they know about, or should they continue learning about what's new to them? Speaking of debate, what about that? Would that kind of forum work once in a while?

The agenda on the board was a comfortable piece. The evening flowed without our feeling pressed about time — it was perfectly segmented. I also feel that our own curriculum is balanced, not too full and not too lean. However, at 8:40 (I wrote the time down) we were back on the decision-making merry-go-round. There are only two ways to stop it. I am a creature of habit and used to a leader stopping and starting "things." Therefore, I was frustrated when we all rode out our final planning about which plan to adopt. I wasn't tired or anxious about time — I just wanted to get to the point, get a plan, any plan.

Perhaps something I will gain from the ETP program is an understanding of the benefits of groups who make their own decisions. On paper the benefits make sense. Being *in* it is different — there is no frustration and confusion on paper.

Rosario raised a question about the relationship between our personal selves and our professional selves. She had noticed that it was difficult for us to decide which topics to study. Perhaps this happened because our personal opinions about what was important to teaching were so strong. We each wanted the seminar to address our personal needs in the classroom. Since our experiences were so varied, it was difficult for us to reach consensus on any one topic. Rosario related this to our classroom practice, which prompted us to ask each member to reflect on how much of their personal lives entered into their teaching. The remaining journal entries reflect this question.

> *Rosario:* [We] can all dig deep into our understanding of what it is that we bring into class and why we do it, which probably could connect to our next session on motivation: Probably a lot of our inner world is what most encourages or frightens both us and our students into good teaching and learning. . . . But let me think of nice examples: Not too long ago, I fell in love . . . and my eyes suddenly seemed to have a different glow, my walking pace became a bit lighter, and I tended to be amused by the silliest anecdotes. My students felt I was more attentive and were bewildered by all the jokes that would occur to me in class. One of them caught me in the corridor and said: "Hey, Rosario, what's up with you, your classes now are more fun, we're really having a ball. Even your comments on our papers are more amusing. Are you in love by any chance" (although that sounded like an improbable situation for a 15-year-old thinking of someone who could almost triple her age), "or what . . . got into you?" I had thought my students enjoyed history. I then discovered that by my being happier, they also felt more enthusiastic about "my" subject matter.

> *Tracey:* We are only human, we have our own lives, and sometimes things happen. What I do about it is to acknowledge it and move on. Let me explain.
>
> Last year, I served as senior adviser, a position which ultimately required all of my school time when I was not teaching and much of my home time as well. It was an extremely frustrating position—all kinds of problems came up, and I spent a lot of time meeting with the principal. Occasionally, I would have to rush to teach a class after some sort of incident that had upset me, and I was obviously upset. My way of dealing with this was to simply tell my students, "I had a rough meeting, give me a few minutes to get myself together." They

never asked for more—they respected what I had said, and the lesson would get underway.

I think they respected me in that way because they knew I would do the same for them. When a student was having a noticeably difficult time or was clearly upset, I left the student alone, meaning I did not pressure the student. This doesn't mean that kids could get away with all kinds of things in my class because they were upset or had a rough home life. For example, several times I have looked at the class and seen a student with tears rolling down his or her cheeks. Without calling attention to the situation, I would wander over quietly and say, "Are you OK? Would you like to go get yourself together, or would you prefer to just hang out here?" Sometimes students would come up to me and say they hadn't done their work because of some family or personal crisis. I would then make an agreement as to when the homework would be made up: "OK. How about if you hand it in by Friday?"

Jane: I have always identified with children who are different or who live on the margins of society. Perhaps this is why I teach in an urban setting. . . . Marginalization is perhaps best understood by those who have been on the sidelines of society. In connecting my personal life to my professional life, this is the connection I would make, as I grew up in a neighborhood where I was the "only one."

Elissa: During my first year of teaching, a teacher I respected told me I was effective with kids because I was the same person in the classroom as I was outside of it. I think about what she said all the time. Is that true—am I the same in both circumstances? Is that actually effective? Why? Sometimes I feel like I know these answers and sometimes I do not.

Duane: Humor, I believe, is a necessary part of learning and the environment one learns in, as well as an indication that one is able to have perspective. . . . I'm not advocating becoming a clown or a comedian, but I am advocating entering into the joy that learning produces and participating in the reality that there's much to this world, including ourselves, that is simply and not so simply funny.

Chris: I grew up on a farm near Buffalo; nature and interactions of living things were abundant. I was given time to watch and figure things out. I don't remember having any outstanding science teachers; in fact, most of my experience in school with science leaned toward memorization. It was an innate love for the subject that brought me to study it more.

I bring this experience into my classroom — not only love for the subject, but wanting to impart the favorite aspects of my experience (the time to watch and figure things out) to my students.

Jorge: Are we talking about values? About political views? About our philosophy of education? I will talk about the values I bring to the classroom. Like most teachers, I see education as an agent of change. . . .

I have lost hope with most of today's leaders. They have proven to be corrupt and inept. However, the next generation doesn't have to be that way. If we can teach these children to be honest and to think critically, our [Colombia's] future won't be as bleak as it presently is.

Doug: I believe that my situation may be unique this year. In the one class I am teaching this year I feel that I probably bring more of my personal self than my professional self into class (either that or I have lost the ability to distinguish the difference between my personal and professional identity). My class is studying Roman lyric poetry, and my students have great facility and ability to translate Latin; therefore, my Latin expertise, my professional self, is rarely essential to the well-being of the class. Consequently, our discussions about the poems are often personally based. I make a supreme effort in my class to model the kinds of personal contributions that I feel are appropriate for this class; however, I feel that if I want my students to contribute their personal feelings and reflections, I must first be willing to open myself to them. Furthermore, I want my students to feel comfortable coming to me to discuss any other problems they might have. For the students to feel comfortable approaching me, there must be a high level of mutual trust and respect already established. . . .

In addition, I believe that a large part of teaching is imparting the morals and beliefs of the teacher to his or her students. As religion loses significance to many of our students and families become more disjointed, it is the teacher who must take responsibility for imparting morals and principles. To many this philosophy would appear to be subversive and dangerous, but this is the type of education I feel most comfortable with. I try to use Latin or math as a tool to teach students to think independently and to accept unique and different ideas of their classmates and others. Only by introducing my personal beliefs as one way of thinking, not necessarily the right one, can I open my students' eyes to the value of different points of view. . . .

Furthermore, I have found it helpful to inform my students of what is going on in my life as openly and directly as possible; consequently, they know who I am as opposed to guessing and creating rumors and speculation. Once the mystery and speculation concerning their teacher's life disappears, so does their interest and fascination, thereby allowing room for interest and enthusiasm for the class material and in-depth discussion of issues of real importance.

Mark: I don't believe that in the teacher–student–subject relation it is either possible or desirable to divorce oneself completely from what one is saying, how one is interpreting, how one hears, and how one chooses to teach. . . . There are times where it is good to act as a sounding board and enable the students to listen acutely to their own individual and/or communal voices; at other times, it is best for them to hear another voice; and above all it is ideal to have an ongoing exchange. That requires that the teacher participate – and I have never had a problem saying what I think. Where I have learned most in actually teaching, as opposed to being taught, is in the area of listening, both to my own voice (how I sound or what others might think I am saying to them) and to the voices of others. . . .

You must show your passionate interest in ideas to engage [students]; they want to know why I love Homer, but I channel my love of Homer into formulating questions based on their first questions. We come at Homer as a problem together – this is easy because Homer is a problem. The tough part is to find out how it can be their problem.

As an English and history teacher, I make clear right off the bat that I abhor the idea of turning the classroom into a morality lesson or a political rally for a cause. That is not to say I don't think "life" issues – evil, love, justice, death, goodness, prudence, courage, judgment – should be the focus of good humanities teaching. But I don't believe children are adults. There are topics and questions that students should not be forced "to face" in undiluted form; heated intellectual debates about philosophy, hot political questions about race, religious questions and ethical questions – these are best approached not by way of political commentary but by way of meditation on or about texts or stories. This is a tricky business. Sometimes this leads to the vision of the teacher as soothsayer – but the student should view us as questioners, as skeptics who are not given to radical or total skepticism.

Even though we each brought to class a package of different experiences and expectations, we had created a vision for what our year together might look like. We began a constructive discussion that would open many other doors. It looked like Rome had fallen, and actually, a lot was yet to happen.

"Well, I Guess We'll Do Motivation"

Kristin Newton and Eleanor Duckworth

November 18

At the end of the November 4 session, the only thing that remained was to select the facilitators for the next session. Elissa volunteered, and Kris was more or less chosen by Eleanor because she would be able to attend a planning meeting on Veteran's Day, which was a school holiday. Kris felt uneasy about her selection and even more so when she discovered that the session itself conflicted with parent/teacher night at her high school. "I was able to make arrangements to miss the parent/teacher conference time but felt guilty (and coerced) while planning and facilitating the session."

Immediately after their selection as facilitators, Elissa and Kris were faced with their first decision: What topic should they do? In keeping with the bowl model adopted by the group (refer to Figure 2), they thought it was time to move outward to the next bowl and begin addressing the issues involving students. They scanned the four topics in the student bowl; having no strong feelings about any of them, they settled on motivation. Although neither of them felt that either of them had any particular expertise in the area of motivation, it did seem like a worthwhile subject.

On Veteran's Day, Elissa and Kris met with Eleanor, Rosario, Chris, and Mark at a restaurant for breakfast. The discussion that began at an early meal continued long after they were asked to leave. They discussed the last session and ways to provide continuity between the two sessions. Though enthusiastic and eager to get on with the curriculum, Elissa and Kris were unsure what the best structure would be for the lesson and what activities would be most interesting to the group.

After a great deal of discussion, they decided that the goal of the session would be to provide opportunities for everyone to share their experiences as well as to do some small-group problem solving around the issue of motivation. The plan was for each person to bring in an example of a classroom situation involving student motivation. After several examples had been shared in the whole group, two or three would be chosen and discussed further in small groups. We would then come back together and share the main points of our discussions.

Elissa and Kris took great care with the wording of the assignment (see Figure 4). They were very specific about the factors that they wanted the members of the class to consider in their motivation cases. In order for the discussions to be effective, they wanted the members to bring as much information about the situations as possible, such as personality character- istics and school environment. Likewise, in planning the small-group dis- cussions, care was taken in posing the questions so that the mission of the group would be to help the person involved think about the situation from a different point of view. Rather than having the small group trying to

FIGURE 4. Homework Assignment, November 18

Please read *Horace's Compromise* by Ted Sizer (1984), chapter on Motivation

Look over the following T-440 readings as they are also relevant:

"The Virtues of Not Knowing" from *The Having of Wonderful Ideas* by
    Eleanor Duckworth (1987)
"Living in Trees" from *The Informed Vision* by David Hawkins (1974)

Reflections and writings:

I. We would like each of you to consider and write about the following. The writing need not be polished and could be in any form (brainstorming list, map, free-write, etc.). We only ask that you consider these things in detail.
1. Reflect upon yourself as a learner, either when you were the age at which you currently teach, or currently at Harvard. Think about times that you were motivated and times that you were not.
2. Re-create a situation about a student you have taught. Consider relationships, culture, curriculum, school environment, personality, and any other factors you think might be related to the student's motivation. Think specifically about instances in which this student was motivated and instances in which this student was not.
We will ask for two of the student examples to work with more in detail, along with the case of Melissa (in the Sizer reading), around the issue of motivation.

II. We would also like you to come to class with a strategy that you have used that has "worked"/helped in dealing with motivation issues. We will take some time to share them. Please bring these in written form because we would like to use them to begin filling the ideas folder.

brainstorm ways to "fix" the problem, the intention was to help the person involved think about the situation more deeply and to allow the small group an opportunity to discuss the issues that affect motivation.

At the beginning of the session, Elissa and Kris offered some working definitions of motivation:

> Motivation: having interest in pursuing a subject, interest in discovery
> To motivate: prompting someone to do something

The class then discussed the connections between motivation and building a curriculum. The emphasis of the discussion was on the importance of considering the motivation of students when developing curricula.

Sizer's (1992) example of Melissa was used as a catalyst for beginning a discussion of motivation stories from our classrooms:

> Melissa headed toward a desk to the teacher's left, against a wall. . . . Melissa watched all this [a class discussion of a poem] without animation. Her face was not blank, quite; there was ennui, acceptance, a trace of wariness. A question was directed to her. She looked at the teacher with little change in expression. A pause. I don't understand. Romagna repeated the question, kindly, without reproach. Another pause. I don't know. Maybe Donne means. . . . Melissa, speaking slowly, quietly, said something, a phrase using words earlier spoken during the teacher's lecture. It was enough to end the exchange, but not enough to provoke a counterquestion or a follow-up by the teacher. . . . Melissa, however unwittingly, was a master at non engagement. (p. 162)

Members were asked to share their own examples of motivation stories.

> *Doug:* I was intrigued in this class by our unwillingness to tell stories of our successful attempts with motivation at the beginning of class. Were we too shy or too modest? Had we lost the familiarity and comfort established 2 weeks earlier? Or were we just confused about the nature of the discussion?

> *Kris:* I had a very different perception of what people would be bringing to discuss. Most of the scenarios seemed to have been "solved." I was worried that we wouldn't have anything to talk about in the small groups. It was also depressing for me to hear about the success stories. I don't feel like I've had any "success stories" this year. I didn't get anything out of hearing about students who suddenly turned around and became wonderful. (What a selfish thing for me to say!!)

Jorge: I received Pina as a third-grade student. She was very quiet, not shy, just a person of few words. She did well in most of her classes, with the exception of math. She didn't understand or like the subject. . . . We never for a second thought she was stupid, but she couldn't put 5 and 6 together to make 11. I set for myself the challenge of making her understand and like the subject.

I had her in third grade, in fifth grade, and in sixth grade. At the end of sixth grade, she didn't understand most of the concepts and still disliked the subject. We became very good friends, but this is definitely not a success story. I wonder if trying . . . a one-on-one situation . . . would help her. How could I motivate her in the classroom? I still don't know. . . .

I spent so much time thinking about the bright students and the Pinas that I think I neglected the ones in the middle of the road. I wonder if I had any Melissas in my class. Considering that I had 200 students, I must admit that most likely I did have some.

After sharing the stories brought in by members of the group, we divided into three smaller groups. The groups were given the following instructions:

Each group will hear about the student in detail and then will generate questions that it thinks are important to address these problems of motivation/lack of motivation. The purpose is *not* to solve the problem but to consider the many factors connected to the student's motivation. Then each group will address the questions it raised and attempt to respond to them. The group should focus on the following: How would we find out the answers? What would we do with this information?

The groups were also told not to tell the teacher how they might have handled the situation or to ask, "Have you tried . . . ?" The class then broke up into groups based on the discussion that interested them. Two groups discussed specific student cases. One case was one of Chris Whitbeck's middle school students (see Interlude I), and the other was that of Melissa. The third group discussed the motivation chapter from *Horace's Compromise* (Sizer, 1984) in a general sense.

Duane: To hear from Chris the background of the student broke my heart, and I wonder how any such student could engage in school work. They're engaged full-time in just coping with the life they've been given. An area of perhaps further discussion is the emotional component as it relates to motivation. There are students we encounter that are dealing with incredible issues at home—issues that have to captivate the students' minds and prevent them from engaging to any significant degree. I certainly do not believe this is the case in all situations, yet for many I believe it is all too true. How do I help that student?

More and more, through this class I am seeing the need and importance of teacher collaboration. How valuable it is to discuss with colleagues the issues that affect us most and that we care about so deeply. It is unfortunate that our school faculties do not engage (there's that word again) in that role more often. It is surely needed and, I believe, is an essential tool in preventing teacher burnout.

Chris: I knew for a long time that several of my students had motivation issues. Many times before our class, I had lamented about Dennis. . . . Seminar offered me several things that had not previously been available: time to reflect and a group of people who were interested, insightful, yet far enough removed from Dennis to look at the situation in a new light.

Susan: [Suzy] forced those of us in her small group to try to define what we meant by motivation. . . . She helped us to realize and articulate that motivation is not a characteristic. Students do not come to us either motivated or not. It is too easy to write off the "unmotivated ones." Also, to me, it seems equally misguided to focus all of our attention on our ability to "motivate." I believe that we should focus on creating engaging learning experiences and find what excites students. We do not do the motivation, but the activity we design does. If we focus too much on how we motivate, then we start talking about reward systems and personal relationships with students. If we think about what engages young people, then we are talking about instruction. . . .

So what are the universals? I do believe that we are all excited by the process of discovery. We need not focus on rewards and "success versus failure" because the students won't see both as part of the process of exploration. We need them to feel free to fall into puddles, and even to see these "mistakes" as vital opportunities for learning. This is part of why I think that competition can be so unhealthy. . . . I do appreciate Jorge's search for the intensity that seems to come from the competition. As I think about it, I am realizing that the drive is really coming from the challenge. I (too) often create races with the clock or even between small groups. I think that the students are responding to the question inherent in the task: Can they do it? I think that we rise to the occasion when we feel our inner resources being tapped into. There is something exhilarating about struggling with something you are not sure — but think maybe — you can do.

Now of course I am using language here that appeals to me — challenge, exploration, and discovery. . . . What do these opportunities for exploration and discovery look like? How do you create access for everyone — in a group at the same time — into the exciting pursuit of new understanding about everything and anything? . . . There is no one way; there are no right answers.

Elissa: I cannot motivate Liz (an upper-middle-class white athlete) in the same ways that I might be able to motivate Andre (an African American male from a lower-income family). This is somewhat depressing to me, but then I do realize that there are some universals in how we can motivate students just by the nature of us all being human. Too, respect and trust are central to this. When I have a student's trust and respect and she has mine, we can work together toward her own learning. It is more when I feel that I am instructing for the sake of instructing (and I hope I do not do this very often) that I know I have lost, for the time being, most kids with the exception, perhaps, of students who are solely motivated by getting good grades (ugh!).

I was very taken by Ted Sizer's chapter on the case of Melissa. . . . I feel that in many ways I was a "Melissa" (and thus my name became "Elissa"; just kidding!). Anyway, like Melissa, I did not take many risks, I did not push myself to be especially creative, nor did I offer my opinion very often in class. I went to a very competitive, non-nurturing, highly academic school in New York City. I "did well" in my courses and graduated, but I graduated with low self-esteem. . . . If one teacher had taken the time to do that [try to understand me] I would have been at least somewhat better off and maybe would have challenged myself to think in a different way and even learn more because of it and thus be motivated to continue to learn more.

Jane: When discussing Melissa, I found something very relevant to my own teaching. It is so simple, I wonder that I never understood it before — a way to know about my students — talk to them. I don't mean to "just talk" but to converse in a way that I will come to know who they are, all the while searching for a tiny piece that will help me help them become more motivated. And through this interaction, what speaks the loudest is that I (the teacher) care about you (the student) — a motivational force itself. . . .

I am especially interested in the competition piece and "What do losers do with competition?" Are they challenged by losing to try harder, or do they just give up? What does a noncompetitive school setting look like? If we are internally motivated, are we competing with ourselves?

If I consider how different all my students are, is it fair to assume that there is only one type of motivation for them—that everyone should be motivated through internal forces, for the love of it? I want to believe that motivation is most useful when it is from the self, but I don't. I do want to join forces with the internal-motivation thinkers. Readings and others are convincing, but my experience with students tells me otherwise.

Last session has pried me from my tightly fused notions about ways to get my students to want to learn. It's exactly what I hoped ETP would be—a crowbar.

We began the whole-class discussion of motivation in general. One major point of debate was the use of competition in the classroom as a motivator. At times the discussion grew heated.

Tracey: There were some clear differences in opinion, and I enjoyed our brief debate. I wish we had more debating and that people [more often] expressed their differences of opinions, that we had the opportunity to discuss them and delve more deeply into issues. I think Jorge started us on that path with his comment about competition.

Jorge: Well administered, [competition] can be very helpful, especially to motivate children. I'm not saying that it should be used blindly. Nevertheless, I am convinced that in certain instances competition motivates children incredibly. It is unfair to simply call it "behaviorist" and throw it to the garbage.

Duane: Do motivation problems increase with age? My limited observation says "yes." Listening to the class last Thursday only reinforced this opinion, but Jane and I are indeed in the minority (i.e., elementary teachers). Yet I face very few motivation problems with my first and second graders. And I wonder why? I also wonder if these wonder-filled, bright-eyed, inquisitive 7- and 8-year olds will one day walk into some high school classroom with glazed eyes, ask not a single question for six periods, stare blindly out the window, and go through an entire day with their mind in neutral. I pray it will never be!

Burry: My thinking about motivation has evolved from a convergence of many different experiences and considerable thought concerning what my teaching is all about. The first of three experiences is rowing. . . . Crew is an incredibly demanding sport. Winning efforts require crew members to combine a willingness to tolerate and overcome intense pain and great exhaustion while maintaining a high level of concentration and subordinating individual desires and needs to the needs of the crew. . . . Training time cuts into your time for other things and physically beats you up. . . .

And yet given all the reasons not to row, some teams appear to create an atmosphere that inspires in their members a selflessness, a commitment to the team, and a willingness to work and achieve results seemingly beyond their abilities. . . . My college team was such a team, and much of our success was due to the way my coach structured our experience. . . . He coached us sparingly and complimented us even more sparingly. But he inspired us to work hard, to push ourselves beyond the limits we had set for ourselves, and to win. He had high expectations for us and insisted that we have high expectations for ourselves. He insisted on results rather than intentions, and he had little tolerance for excuses. He was willing to show us that he cared for us by respecting us, treating us honorably, holding us accountable for our results, taking the time to listen to us, and occasionally by being willing to give us a swift kick in the backside. He also had fun with us. He wasn't above a good joke. He did goofy, slapstick, human things. And his ridiculous West Virginia twangy laugh would often echo throughout the boathouse. In doing so, he made our school a "dynasty" school in small college rowing.

Doug: Can it be effective to motivate students to do the work even if they are not inspired to learn the material? Are there any topics that students must learn and cannot be taught in a fascinating manner? I have yet to learn how to teach the Latin declinations and conjugations in a way that inspires students to learn these endings and inflections just for the pure love of knowing. I have used games and activities to make the task of learning and drilling fascinating; these important tools are just diversions. I am not making the material itself more interesting. Some methods of teaching Latin have been devised that ignore endings and try to teach students Latin through reading many stories. While these can be interesting for students, the Latin is fictitious, and the students generally are weak at translating ancient texts or understanding the syntax of the materials.

Are there such things as bad motivation strategies? Certainly! I do not want my students feeling that they need to do the work so I won't hit them or so their parents won't hit them. But what about the motivation of competition or the driving force of pleasing one's parents or teachers or the desire to go to a good college? Are these "bad" motivations? Will students with these driving forces lose out on their education? They may not experience the same excitement as students who learn to satisfy their curiosity, but they may be acquiring the tools to become curious or to become able to explore their future interests.

After the large-group discussion, we began what was to become an important group process—the closing circle. At the end of class each week, anyone who wished would have a moment to say anything he or she had not the chance to say. This became a way to see what had moved our classmates the most, what had angered them, what had intrigued them, or, in tonight's case, why some people were quiet. Tonight's sharing focused largely on two things: on the number of motivational issues that we did not discuss and on the fact that we were not yet comfortable as a group.

Duane: Motivation is a key issue—an issue often talked about but an issue that often eludes us. The only thing I would have liked to have added to the discussion was time. The issue was far from solved, and I felt the dialogue was far from exhausted. I wanted more, and yet time didn't allow. And once again, a portion of the issue eludes me.

Chris: In our attempt to offer a chance to those people who are usually quiet, we prevented some members of the group from speaking. This is an issue that I'm sure will continue throughout the year. How do we reach this balance? It is easy to ask someone what they think. It is difficult to tell those who speak too much that they need to be quiet. Once they are quiet, when is it OK for them to share their views again? There needs to be some measure of checks and balances.

It is amazing that in a 3-hour class we run out of time for people to share. As teachers we dream of 3-hour classes. As students in the ETP seminar, we dream of weekly 3-hour seminars instead of biweekly ones.

Doug: I was intrigued by Mark's attempt to participate less in class last night, and I decided to follow his lead. Unfortunately, I was not able to do this by listening more closely to the rest of the class, but instead I became distracted and disengaged with the discussion. I found it difficult to be quiet without being passive. I need to train myself to become an active listener, since I become too involved, rude, and aggressive when I take an active role in a discussion. Then again, at times, I think I am being too aware and analytical of the class dynamics and should just let the class happen without thinking so much about it. . . . I feel it would be more enjoyable just to sit back, relax, and absorb the information as it is being presented.

Mark: I enjoyed the opportunity to test myself to see if I could be silent without appearing to be too contrived or stand-offish. . . . I was sorry that Burry didn't get a chance to explain his chart of dates that his classes made. Here was an example of a direct attempt at motivation that was concrete. We could have developed questions from this. It was unfortunate that he did not assert this as much as he could have as a possibility for 15 minutes of dialogue. Perhaps we are too wrapped up in this anxiety about schedules and "getting things done."

Jorge: I would like to have another class about motivation. There are more stories, and there are other aspects to discuss. I think we can have some great discussions in this class. The more I get to know the people, the clearer [become] the differences between them.

There is a definite revolution in education. There is a new way of looking at students, teachers, classrooms, evaluations—in short, everything. However, I get the impression that people who ascribe to progressive education consciously or unconsciously ignore many helpful aspects of traditional education.

Tracey: I'm not sure that we came to any sort of conclusion about motivation, but I am comfortable with that because I think the topic will continue to reappear, starting with the session Susan and I are planning on cooperative learning. I do wish we had talked about the "Melissa" case as a large group, because so many of us have Melissas. The Melissas slide by, and the scariest part of all that is it is so easy as a teacher to let that happen because the others already take more time than you have.

Elissa: Many of the issues I deal with every day as a teacher came right back to me on Thursday night—how do you keep most or everyone engaged? How do you help all of them feel included and comfortable and invested, and how do you find the right balance between talking and not talking so that you can be an effective guide and facilitator? . . . On Thursday, I felt that I could have guided more. This brings up the issue of team facilitation. I think that having both of us guiding each discussion is a great idea, but I recognize even more so now some of the issues within team teaching. How does one facilitate without stepping on another's toes? How do you find comfort and ease within team teaching, while at the same time providing a challenging and interesting class for your students/peers?

In writing this account, Kris came to realize that she embodied, that evening, many of the motivation issues raised in this session.

Kris: I do not quite know what to think about last night's session. It has been a very long week, and I have had a lot on my mind, so I was already a bit distracted when I came to class. I also didn't have very much energy. One of my classes has been getting more and more difficult. I have been reaching them less and less frequently. They have begun to insult me behind my back, and it is very demoralizing. Yesterday was particularly bad in that respect. So it had been a lousy day. I was also stressed out about facilitating and watching the time in the session. . . . I was worried that people would feel cheated if we didn't get to everything that we had talked about doing. . . . I didn't enjoy [the session] very much. I did not get much out of it in terms of the topic of motivation. I don't know if that was because I was distracted or because I was worried about facilitating. I thought about whether I would have enjoyed the session had I not been facilitating it. I had not considered that during the planning process. Instead I had focused on the rest of the class. I wish we had more time to share our ideas. . . . I remember very little about the large-group discussion beyond the debate about competition and its place in teaching. That aspect was mildly interesting to me, but I didn't feel at all involved in it.

One of the issues that this session highlights is that adult groups often have the same problems that are typically attributed to a certain group of students, in this case, lack of motivation. In some ways such problems are more serious in adult groups because adults are more likely to tolerate them or politely brush them off as unimportant. Kids, on the other hand, are more likely to make their feelings known; this takes our attention away from the difficulties of the situation and permits us to attribute it to difficulties of individual students. Perhaps there is much we can learn from ourselves that is applicable to our own young students.

Against All Odds: Creating Possibilities for Children to Invent and Discover

CHRISTOPHER WHITBECK

ETP allowed Chris the opportunity to reflect on and share his classroom experiences with Dennis and motivation. This paper is a product of his reflecting on his classroom practice via writing conferences with Suzy Ort.

Dennis is angry, a time bomb waiting to explode. Sometimes he is intimidating, both to other students and to me. It's easy to see that he does not want to be in school. There are other students who do a task when asked, contribute during group work, but do only the minimum needed to get by. Although with different manifestations, it is clear that both types of students are uninterested in class. Even when presented with some materials that other students find very interesting, it is difficult to get either excited about learning, as I recorded in my journal:

> The waterwheel was spinning with tremendous force. It lifted 50 large nails quickly. Water was splashing everywhere, and the students were cheering loudly as the competition to see whose wheel would lift the most nails drew to a near photo finish. Dennis sat stoically on the side of the room. Physically and emotionally removed from the rest of the class, his "I don't care if we win or lose" attitude was not different from that displayed in any other activity that he had been forced to participate in this year. (5/1/93)

David Hawkins (1974) wrote, "Students are not given nearly enough time to just wander and sniff in the academic maze" (p. 176). He tells about experimental groups of learners who do much better when given time to explore freely. I believe that he's right. Allowing students time to investigate and "mess about" with materials, giving them time to see how things work, is better than pressuring them to hit the books and come up with an immediate answer. But as my journal reflections from this year will show, I do not see my students become more motivated just because I give them more time.

> Just giving time to enjoy the maze doesn't sit right. I don't think that giving my students more time to discover would provide any more motivation to enjoy the experience. I would still have the students who were uninterested within the course of half an hour. The easily distracted student, the student who goes for the obvious answer and does not want to *work* toward the explanation – these would be no more motivated given more time to feel comfortable with the maze. These students would sit in a corner of the maze and draw pictures on the wall. Although this may be a form of learning and self-expression, it is not valuable to the creation of critical thinking skills as I see them. (10/16/93)

I know that there is more to wanting to learn than just giving students time. As a graduate student studying education, teaching full-time, as well as attending classes, I am very attuned to what really happens in the classroom. I'm constantly thinking of applying techniques being modeled at the graduate school to the classes that I teach. Motivating students to do the work needed to discover new ideas is a challenging task. It involves tapping into a student's reserved stores of energy. At the core of the motivation problem is wonder. I want my students to wonder – to want to find answers. I want them to use all of their energy investigating their ideas. People in my graduate school classes expect that the willingness of students to invest this energy will be automatic if interesting problems are presented in the manner in which they have been modeled during our graduate classes. I have evidence to the contrary.

> The eighth grader who is "just getting through" science class is not vested in solving the problem. . . . I have a science class of eighth-grade students that is homogeneously grouped. It includes all of the low-achieving students, while all of the "good" students are in the other . . . I hate this arrangement. It produces what I call the class from hell. . . .
> Eleanor [Duckworth, 1987] has written in her book that "Schools and teachers can provide materials and questions in ways that suggest things to be done with them; and children, in the doing, cannot help being inventive" [p. 7]. In the case of this eighth-grade class, I've come to believe that this is not true. . . . I pose questions to children with a genuine interest in having them mess about with materials and seeing

what works. In short I encourage student's divergent ideas and provide a setting and materials that hopefully encourage wonderful ideas.

Why don't these students have wonderful ideas? . . . Dennis is afraid. His home life hints of abuse, neglect, drug abuse, and humiliation. He has learning disabilities and is angry at the world. The last thing he is going to try is telling the class some crazy idea he has about why sand loses volume when it gets wet. He has shut down. Dennis hides behind a mask of anger, belligerence, and avoidance. He can be accepted by laughing at the wrong moments and disrupting class with his friends. Nowhere in Dennis's life has a wonderful idea ever been rewarded or encouraged except in school. I feel both anger and sadness toward Dennis. (9/30/93)

I wonder what the rest of Dennis's life is like. If it's as unpleasant as I imagine, I don't think that his 8 hours of school can begin to outweigh 16 hours of lack of respect in an environment that discourages wonderful ideas. David Hawkins (1974) wrote, "To have respect for children is more than recognizing their potentialities in the abstract, it is also to seek out and value their accomplishments" (p. 48). I do this. There is nothing more exciting to me than a student who struggles through an idea and makes some discoveries. I present my class with problems that invite investigation. I share my enthusiasm as they form ideas, and the pleasure shines across both of our faces when every piece of data, every observation, and a sea of unorganized thoughts finally come together. Like a marathon runner addicted to the "highs" of running a long race, the pleasure and enjoyment of finding things out can be addictive. I value these experiences and believe strongly that parents must be held accountable for the same. In my utopian world I would like Dennis to find a refuge in school and gain strength from his success in class. His desire to test ideas and experience the "rush" that accompanies the moment when you discover an answer would overcome anything else that was happening in his life, but this is not going to happen.

"Exploratory behavior dominates only in the absence of other more urgent need" (Hawkins, 1974, p. 184). I wrote about this in a journal entry in October. Knowing that there was only so much that I could offer students who didn't want to learn has become frustrating. Teaching is more than filling vessels, but students like Dennis wouldn't even look at the tools that they could use to fill the vessel. There would be no way that they would work toward a greater understanding of the material about which I was trying to get them to think.

We have primary drives that motivate us — hunger, sex, and pain.
Learning mechanisms should be added to the primary motivations.

These learning mechanisms may only be expressed when the other drives are fulfilled.

This has much to say about the effects of the "abusive" home life. My students, with whom I am concerned and sometimes angered, are not having primary drives satisfied. Hawkins does not give me answers but provides more insight as to what is causing the problem. I agree that learning is a primary motivation; this also gives me hope toward motivating my students to actively learn. (10/16/93)

Overall, I believe that only a given percentage of any person's effort can be given to learning. Much of our energy is given toward surviving. Daily struggles have a great effect on the motivation of many people, adolescents in particular. How can they concentrate on learning when they must worry about being emotionally or physically beaten outside of school?

In response, I have spent much of my semester catching Dennis at doing good things. When Dennis makes a critical observation and mumbles it under his breath, I share what I hear with the class and point out how important his contribution was. Dennis makes faces when I do this; he wouldn't want people to think that he knows something—that ain't cool! And yet his special education teachers report that he is very pleased, that his face shines when he adds to class or when he gets a good grade on a science test. I do not sugar coat my comments for Dennis. I only point out what I see as a true success.

Dennis has had moments of motivational change, and at times he has worked well during the semester. I wonder how much of my interaction with Dennis has had an effect on his participation and behavior. In my science class there are three emotionally or behaviorally challenged students; all of them have trouble dealing with the positive reinforcement that I offer. When they begin to do well or get continual positive reinforcement, they break down, withdraw, and sabotage their own success. If Dennis has handed in a week's worth of assignments and is not only passing science class but may be edging toward a *B*, he immediately stops working. I will see no work for the next week, and behavior problems will reappear. Small pieces of paper begin to fly across the room, strange noises can be heard, and other students begin yelling that so and so hid their book bag or crumpled their science homework. Just enough disruption to make the teacher want to isolate or reprimand someone. Dennis can always be found at the center of these disruptions. He gets in trouble, misses work, and his grades begin to slip. It's as though he cannot handle the "rush" of success. He is afraid to become addicted to this because it is not always within his reach. For Dennis and other students like him, it is easier to avoid this rush-causing experience than to become addicted to something that you know is very hard to obtain.

I have also noticed that a student like Dennis is often entrenched in feelings of failure. Dennis is in eighth grade but failed seventh-grade science. The moments of success he has had this year let me know that he is capable of very advanced thinking and is very qualified to complete difficult work. This is challenging to Dennis. He would not want me to become dependent on him for ideas or expect him to get all of his work done. Being depended on is not something that Dennis feels he can handle. Remember, Dennis is using much of his energy just to keep his anger in check and survive each day; he doesn't have the extra energy to support the other students in science class by sharing ideas and becoming involved in a discussion. In addition, thinking is hard work, and it is easier for Dennis to hide behind his past failures than to work at solving a problem. Some students say that they are bored when class becomes challenging; Dennis and other students like Dennis who are looking for an excuse that will get them out of working hard say, "Why should I even try? I'm going to fail anyway!"

Providing materials and questions in ways that suggest things be done with them often leads to children's inventive, interesting action. If students are not familiar with the work that accompanies these materials and questions, they become confused, frustrated, and bored. It takes practice and determination to become a good thinker. One class a day will not provide the time to master this skill. It takes many classes and many weeks, months, or years for it to become "uncool" to share ideas. It will take the same number of creative teachers and interesting, thought-provoking classes to build these thinking skills to the level that I see in some of the students from a kindergarten class I visited this year.

Thinking is hard work, but I believe that neither an abusive home life, peer pressure, adolescent identity seeking, nor stolen voices can overcome the determination of a dedicated team of talented teachers trying to prepare their students for the much harder thinking that will be demanded by life outside of school. This should be the teacher's mission. One teacher in a school of many cannot overcome all of these obstacles. We need teams of teachers working cooperatively, creating a safe environment that demands and motivates our students to work toward understanding. We need to value their questions and their voices. As Piaget wrote, "The goal in education is not to increase the amount of knowledge, but to create the possibilities for a child to invent and discover" (quoted in Hawkins, 1974, p. 188). We can only foster invention and discovery by providing the right materials, the time to work with these materials, the listening ear and watchful eye that try to understand what the student is thinking about these experiences. This cannot be done in the vacuum of one room within a larger school.

Only a dedicated team of teachers working together to create an environment for children to invent and discover will be able to overcome the many obstacles that lie in the way of our students' understanding.

Dennis has not changed much during the school year. There have been moments of success and moments of failure. In May, Dennis had decided that he was not going to pass science, and he stopped handing in all work. The work that he did hand in was always handed in without a name—it was as if he wanted the feedback that I give on papers but did not want to have this success to be attributed to him. He participated in no activities, and any conversation that I had with him seemed to amount to nothing. He will probably fail the marking period and the year.

This comes on the tail of one of his most successful marking periods. If I am taking responsibility for some of Dennis's success, I must also review my role in his failures. This roller-coaster ride tires both of us. I'm afraid that we'll get to a point where neither of us wants to try anymore. I am left wondering if he will ever experience the joy of learning. It doesn't feel as if the things I did made a difference in his life this year. I wish I knew.

Eye to Eye

TRACEY GUTH

December 2

Susan and I deliberately planned this session on cooperative learning to be unlike the class meetings we had experienced so far. When we first met to plan the session, we agreed that the group had spent a lot of time in discussion; we wanted to shake things up and do something different. It was time to move around, to be active, to experiment with ideas and be creative. In short, we wanted to play.

We began with a homework assignment asking each person to bring five objects that we planned to have them use in the creation of an ideal school. During our planning session, the exact wording of this simple request actually occupied us for over 30 minutes: We did not want to plant ideas in anybody's minds by being too suggestive, nor did we wish to be unclear or limiting, a dilemma often inherent in lesson planning. Our final instructions for this task were as follows: "Please bring five objects that you believe make up the ideal school. You can be as literal or symbolic as you want. Be prepared to share them with the others in the group."

We meant to accomplish several goals with the "creating an ideal school" activity: On one hand, we wanted to be physically active by working to build something, to provide an opportunity for some fun, and, most important, to shift from being in the role of teachers; we wanted each person to really experience cooperative learning *as students*, and then to use that experience as the basis for discussion. Realistically, though, we knew it was impossible to have a group of teachers such as ours totally divorce themselves from that identity. So, on the other hand, we chose an activity that allowed room for expression as teachers in order to bring in our thoughts about schools and schooling. This activity also reflected our particular interpretation of cooperative learning: a situation which provides an opportunity for learning, discussion, and creativity while everyone is actively involved. Our goal was to experience the kind of learning that can occur in a small group.

Continuing in the vein of shaking things up, we resolved that this session would start *on time*, as we had noticed a trend to begin later and later each week. Promptly at 6:00, we began an icebreaker activity, despite the absence of some who had to figure out what was happening when they eventually did arrive. Everyone was to line up in order of eye color, lightest to darkest. This prompted lots of laughing accompanied by deep looks into each other's eyes (and complaints about the room's lighting). We then formed three groups by dividing the line into thirds.

In each group, people explained their objects to each other. After their initial object presentations, the groups were instructed as follows: "Using the materials your group members brought and the supplies provided (index cards and tape), build your group's vision of the ideal school." As with the homework assignment, these instructions were carefully worded so as not to in any way lead the groups down a certain path.

Our classmates did not disappoint us in their choices of objects and the ideas they represented. Each group shared their objects together and then spent an intense but entertaining period "constructing" their visions of an ideal school. As their ideas of a school differed, so did their use of the objects. One group highlighted the importance of access to schools. They created a circular structure containing many openings with a courtyard in the middle. The rest of their objects were placed in the middle and included such items as a rock, a prescription drug container meaning knowledge, an Almond Joy candy bar representing joy, four cut-out paper *C*'s (caring, creativity, curiosity, and community), a compass, a picture book to symbolize learning (which is fun and colorful), a nonthreatening teddy bear, and a patterned scarf standing for the ideas of interdisciplinary curriculum and diversity. Two members of the group had even brought the same object — recordings of Aretha Franklin's song "Respect."

The objects for another group included a hand-bell, Latin book, flashlight, weight, mechanical toy, and umbrella. They set a goal of using everyone's objects as part of the physical structure of a school. They changed the meanings of objects as necessary: a weight, originally meant to signify the idea of depending on others, came to represent science. They hung the umbrella open from the ceiling in such a way that it spun freely, with the other objects either attached to the umbrella or arranged underneath.

After the activity, we wanted to draw on that immediate experience to bring out some features of cooperative learning. The groups remained together and considered these questions:

1. How well did you achieve what you set out to do? Be sure to discuss how you feel about your model, as well as how you worked together as a group.
2. Did you ever have an idea that either you did not express or was not heard by others? Were you ever aware of someone else presenting an idea that was overlooked?

3. What role did each person play? If you could play a different role,
   what would it be? What can others do to help you achieve that role?
4. How could you improve as a group?

According to the agenda, the small-group activities would be followed
by a break and a large-group discussion, but we made an impromptu decision to follow the break with group presentations of their schools. Everyone
was so enthusiastic that it would have been impossible to just dismantle the
models and move on. We could not settle down for discussion until we
knew what the spinning umbrella meant, not to mention how it worked. It
became clear that the process of working in a group had as much importance as the products being created, and when looking back at the experience, that process became, for some, more memorable than the schools
created. Journal entries indicate that many people not only enjoyed themselves but, as we had hoped, also found that the activity was a good way of
addressing issues of cooperative learning and schooling in general.

Jane: Thinking of five objects was easy, for they represented things I
don't have and have often wished were a part of my school life: time,
space, fewer interruptions, ways to make the classroom belong to my
students, and collegiality. . . . Collegiality was my top priority. Of
course I do not mean teachers who go out socially, but teachers who
are honest, open, willing to share their ideas, and be helped by others
who may be able to offer insights into difficult moments. I mean administrators who invite and accept comments and criticism from their
staff. In a nutshell, a group who learns from each other through the
sharing of ideas.

Susan: For me, the whole atmosphere and tone of the course shifted
as we sat down at our small table. Although it is important to study
when and why cooperative learning breaks apart, I want to focus for a
moment on our small group's cohesion. We experienced a collective
creative process that is worth trying to understand. As each person in
turn arranged their carefully chosen objects in front of them, and began to speak with mounting pride and passion, I watched and felt the
rest of us leaning closer, straining to absorb the presenter's thoughts
and being. As my turn approached, I wondered why I was beginning
to feel uncomfortable. . . . It seems to me that in our society it can be
unsettling to be listened to so carefully because we are not used to it. I
suddenly realized how little experience we have listening as well as being listened to. As I continued my presentation, I found myself speaking softly, clearly, confidently, and succinctly. I felt heard, valued,

able to be myself, and therefore open to and immersed in the experience. And I felt a part of something larger than myself.

Doug: While we were fanciful, symbolic, and playful, I think that we built a school that could work and be extremely successful. It was fun to watch a bunch of "cynics" have fun with idealism and fantasy despite all of our complaints of the separation from reality that we find in many of our [Harvard] classes. It was fascinating to watch my group wrestle with the ways that our idealistic strategies could work in our [schools].

Duane: It was not only challenging to think of the five objects but even more challenging integrating them with others into a creative whole. I enjoyed the challenge, but it was not an easy process. . . . Our group created not only a valuable model/product but a dynamic that I believe is illustrative of what cooperative learning is all about. It is about all participating, all engaged (and engaging one another to deeper thinking), all listening, all responsive, and all taking credit for the final product. Our model would not have looked like it did if any one of us had been absent (or idle). It was a wonderful group-learning process.

Elissa: Whereas I tend to be quiet and hesitant to talk in larger groups (even our ETP group), I felt comfortable to be a vocal part within our group of five. I think there are several layers behind this: the trust that was established from the beginning in offering our objects, my group's willingness to listen and be respectful, and my own engagement and interest in the activity at hand. All of this brings me to think about cooperative learning and how important these components could be to what we do in our classes.

After the presentations of the models, Susan and I resumed our original plan by beginning a large-group discussion. Rather than discussing cooperative learning in general or classrooms in which we have taught, we turned to the specific topic of our ETP class as a cooperative learning group. We made this decision because we felt that the class had all become very aware of "the group." "The group" was becoming a topic of as much interest as those the class had chosen earlier: motivation, curriculum, assessment. Here is how we drafted our introduction to that discussion:

We hope that the activity and discussion have raised thoughts and questions about how groups work and the roles people play. We thought that we could now take this opportunity to look at and discuss ourselves as a large group. How well do we function as a group? What roles do people play? How have we changed as a group?

The agenda also included an "Analysis and Applications Discussion," but it was planned for the end of class, to take place only if time allowed. We realized that some group members might be unhappy at not having the opportunity to discuss cooperative learning in the context of their classrooms, but the functioning of "the group" seemed just as important. Of course, time did not allow—the first part of the large-group discussion lasted until the end of class, and there never was time to talk about cooperative learning as we had or had not used it. Those who felt a need to discuss cooperative learning in their classrooms found a way through their journals, while almost all the group members commented further on "the group." The general trend toward increased openness and comfort within the group also reflected a new willingness to disagree with each other's ideas.

Kris: When I first got the homework assignment about bringing in objects that represent our ideal school, I resented it. I don't want to talk about an ideal school. I want to talk about my school, and my classroom, and my students. I must say I did get into finding the objects. I reflected upon my perception of my school, and that was valuable. . . . I did very much enjoy the small-group work. . . . I was very proud of what we had done. After the small-group work, we had a great discussion about the dynamics of our class. . . . But the same thing happened that always happens. We didn't get to talking about our own classes.

Chris: You cannot plop students into a group and expect them to automatically work cooperatively. . . . Given the right group, and I stress this idea, the most uninvolved student can learn something. Often we teachers do not take the time to find out what this student learned. If my group did not value my participation, if they tried to complete the task and never involved me, I would not have learned as much. I see a true value within cooperative learning that I did not see before.

Suzy: Our small-group debriefing and large-group discussion reminded me of how important it is to process cooperative learning activities. What did we do? How was it? How did it feel? What roles do people play, etc. . . . My experience, however, has been that the "debriefing," where "process analysis" is addressed, often gets pushed out as frivolous in favor of getting whatever task accomplished. I definitely struggle with this in my own classroom not because I don't value the group process but because there seems to be a distinction in my mind between the activity, the academics, and the processing of the activity. . . . When I first started at University Heights, I really thought that it was, in a word, weird. We devoted a lot of staff meeting time to us, the teachers—how we functioned as a group. At any given moment, one person would say, "I don't feel comfortable with . . . " and the group would turn to them trying to analyze what was going on and how to deal with whatever it was. My first reaction was often, "Deal with it on your own if you can't see where the group is going. Don't take up our time selfishly." I also wondered why everyone else seemed to be "catering" to this person who was slowing us down, as I saw it. . . . At the same time, it also felt kind of familiar and somehow I knew that once I got used to it, I would find it OK. . . .

I came to see them as meetings where there was a very positive, accepting, and supporting atmosphere. They were a safe (and by no means always polite, yet always respectful) place to take risks. And I learned that in the practice of group process I became more adept at articulating my feelings and my thoughts not only about the group but also about a given subject. I started to feel like I could better "put my finger on things," understand things because I had new skills in articulation, discussion, and questioning. In this way, I began thinking about how to get those lessons into my classes along with American history.

Elissa: Thursday's class also reminded me to think about the roles kids take on in groups and the types of climate that are conducive to cooperative learning in classrooms. . . . The teacher, I think, must communicate the values of trust, open-mindedness, and honesty and *be* it— act that way, live that way so the kids can see it. Our students need to explore different roles for themselves, and in this open, nurturing environment they can take those risks that help them grow and learn and also facilitate cooperative learning.

Jane: I feel our large-group discussion may represent a turning point in the ETP program. It was the first time we discussed things that are uncomfortable. I feel that an important piece of group dynamics is to surface discomfort. It brings forth honesty and, in turn, trust. There is a link between self-disclosure and the dynamics of the group. But I see it as a way to know who we are, as well as a way to know that what we say will be valued, although (hopefully) not always met with agreement.

Doug: I would love to discover how we can encourage people to say exactly what they are thinking. . . . I have enough faith and confidence in the talent of this group to assume that when I disagree with a statement it is understood that my disagreement lies with the sentiment, not with the individual; however, maybe these ground rules need to be reestablished. One of the goals I had for my year at graduate school was to have the opportunity to discuss various elements of teaching—I do not want to be told everything I do is great and wonderful, nor do I want to feel compelled to accept everything I hear as the perfect solution. I am eager and willing to defend what I do in my classroom so I can be convinced that I could be doing things better.

Chris: Debate is the lifeblood of new ideas. We will never enter a new level of understanding, our ideas and philosophies will not evolve, we will leave as the same teachers who entered the seminar if we are not challenged. Much like our students, our ideas, our structures will not simply change because we have been presented with new ideas.

Mark: I was curious to see . . . when we got together in a larger group to talk about our "class" group dynamic, that some people were feeling I was unhappy or stifled when I was "clamming up." . . . I have been trying to keep my thinking aloud inside, and I have tried to curb my instinct to speak, so I might listen more and respond more accurately. I will do this as much as my instincts tell me to do, but I won't curb or change my nature. So I just don't want people in the class to worry too much, though I appreciate the concern for my well-being.

Duane: Our large-group discussion about ourselves was timely. We really had not done this to date, but I think we need to do this from time to time. I agree with Jane that we are indeed "polite," yet we are a group of teachers, and the teachers I most respect are polite and respectful (as Aretha challenges us to be). Although I believe we could be more challenging, directed, probing, exhorting, and questioning of one another, I think there's a good reason we are not at this point in the semester. I frankly don't believe we really know each other well enough to do that and to be that for one another. . . . If relationally we are to go "deeper" and further, . . . polite, I believe, is exactly what we should be with/to one another.

The openness of the group was a significant change because it was a vital step toward the goal that brought us together in the first place—the opportunity to reflect on our individual experiences as teachers. The right balance of politeness, respect, and debate is necessary for such reflection.

> *Rosario:* Personally, the politeness of the group has been a really interesting learning experience. . . . I feel I have never been in such a truly respectful environment where I have an honest and sincere regard for what each person has to say. This sincerity is what allows me to be able to reflect on what I actually do in my classroom, because sometimes I feel that I can become very defensive when any of my deep beliefs on teaching are challenged. I don't know why the way I think I teach is so precious to me. It is as if it were part of my identity. It is what I put all my thoughts and energy into. If I come to realize that I haven't been doing as wonderful a job as I thought I had, it can be very depressing. That's why I feel that the atmosphere has to be indeed as positive as we have been building it. . . . In that sense I am looking forward to our next meeting on assessment because that's where I feel my biggest inconsistencies will flourish; and as I said before, I feel no problem in exploring all the reasons I have for doing things the way I do them within a group of respectful people as interested as I am in understanding why we teach the way we do.

We seemed to reach a consensus—not only that cooperative learning was an invaluable classroom tool but also that we were making great strides as a group. We began to challenge and question one another and to be truthful about our differences in viewing schools. We were beginning to understand that, while we looked into each other's eyes, we were not necessarily seeing eye to eye.

Assessing Assessment

SUZY ORT

December 16

In the session that Doug and I led, we hoped to launch a spirited discussion about one of education's hottest topics, that of student assessment. As we planned, we were conscious of time constraints. Among other things, the group wanted to celebrate the coming holidays (and vacation!), and we were organizing a small gift-giving ceremony. We wanted to structure our session so that the conversation, rather than being largely theoretical or abstract — how assessment should be done in the ideal, all that is wrong with the omnipresent letter grade — would consider the problems and promises of alternative forms of assessment. We set the stage by including readings about student exhibitions from Ted Sizer's (1992) *Horace's School* in our homework assignment (see Figure 5).

FIGURE 5. Homework Assignment, December 16

I. Read the following excerpts from *Horace's School* (Sizer, 1992): pp. 102–117, pp. 23–27, pp. 48–49, pp. 65–66, pp. 79–81, pp. 98–101, pp. 118–119, pp. 133–134. (Copies of these pages available in our drawer.)

II. Bring in the titles of any other suggested readings on the topic of assessment by Tuesday, December 14, 4:00 PM so we can create a suggested reading list by Thursday.

III. Buy for less than a dollar or make in less than half an hour a present for the person assigned to you. You will find an envelope in our drawer with your name on the outside and your assigned person inside. Please be creative and have fun with this assignment. Please wrap the present and put the recipient's name on the outside, since these presents will be handed out anonymously at the end of class on Thursday.

We decided to orchestrate a role-play of a school board meeting. We thought that our group, faced with a hypothetical situation, would grapple with the thorny issues of assessment. Each class member was assigned a different role to play at the school board meeting — board member, superintendent, teacher, school principal, guidance counselor (college adviser), parent, or, finally, recalcitrant student. The question before the board was: Should district schools switch from traditional *A* through *F* report cards and transcripts to an assessment system that relies almost solely on narrative descriptions of a student's skills and understandings over the course of a high school career? Examples of each assessment system, from real high schools, were provided to the committee for review.

> *Chris:* Usually I dread role-play, . . . [but] I enjoyed the opportunity to freely present a position that I would not usually present. There are usually many ideas that I want to share with the group on any given night. Because we are always concerned about time, I would not share something that is not important to me for fear that what I feel is most important might go unsaid. The role-play made me focus on these ideas that usually would have slipped by.

> *Duane:* I thought the role-play not only was fun but also helpful in uncovering the complexity of the issue.

During the role-play, many "school board members" asked the group to consider the fundamental purposes of assessment — why do we "do" assessment? Is the primary purpose of assessment essentially "diagnostic" in that it should help teachers understand, through some kind of symbolic representation, what students know and can do? Or is the purpose of assessment to act as a conduit for giving feedback to students about their work?

> *Elissa:* As a student I was evaluated with comments in grade school, and then abruptly in seventh grade I received grades without comments. Why did this change occur? All of a sudden I could be evaluated by one letter rather than a page of comments about examples of what I had accomplished and what I might need to work on. This seems ridiculous and criminal to a child's sense of herself. How it must feel to think that your work and efforts and ideas can be judged and communicated by one letter!!!
>
> In the school where I teach, we send home, along with grades, a half-page of comments five times a year with grades to the child and her parents; yet the colleges only want the grades. . . . Why is this? Why do our schools, at least for grades 7–12, buy into this and only

grade our students without much comment? How can we expect the
students to learn if they do not get any feedback? How do we feel, as
students this year, if we get a paper or exam back that offers only a letter or number grade. I would feel like my ideas were not valued very
much and that I did not say anything good enough, interesting
enough, or bad enough to be worth reacting to or commenting on.

Susan: I think that I am learning the most here [at graduate school]
about education from being a student. Right now, having handed in a
variety of assignments, I am waiting — with anticipation — to hear back
from a couple of my courses about my performance. What I crave is
not judgment but response. Teachers often see grades as an important
reward system; it is reward enough to be responded to. I do not need
to know what a teacher thinks of me; I need to know that a teacher
thinks with me.

To Elissa and Susan, assessment is the formalized system of giving feedback
to students. They also suggest that assessment should inform practice —
both teachers' teaching practices and students' learning practices.

Burry focused on assessment from the teacher's perspective. For him,
assessment should represent a systematizing of a teacher's thoughts about
"what do I want children to walk away with?"

Burry: I feel that assessment tools should be both opportunities for
the teacher to receive feedback on the efficacy of his or her teaching
strategies, and opportunities for students to take accountability for
their learning. . . .
    When I first started teaching, I planned a lot of activities that
were creative and fun and possibly even effective. And then I would
sit back and scratch my head and wonder how I would assess the darn
things.
    The question is "bass ackwards." One should not say "what do I
want the students to do?" as if children were circus animals who could
learn from the hoops that they are made to jump through. Rather one
should begin with "what do I want the children to learn and walk away
with?" . . . Knowing what one wants one's students to learn at the outset almost automatically sets up the assessment strategy.

Automatic, perhaps not. Tough, it is. How can teachers comment, give
feedback, respond, either in narrative form or with a symbolic representation such as *A*'s, *B*'s and *C*'s, while also encouraging students to explore

and discover their own understandings? Are grades more objective than narrative?

Susan: It is ironic to me that we claim that grades are more objective and yet they feel so judgmental. If they were objective, they would merely be illuminating. The reality is that no pronouncement can be objective, and therefore we must honestly work with our subjectivity. I think that comments are more honest and potentially more instructive. It is easy to fear that comments are just too subjective, but they do not have to be character statements. Narratives can and should be as specific as possible, not about who the student is but about what the student has done.

Elissa: The issue of assessment is a difficult one for many reasons. One that I think about often is how it interferes or can interfere with building a classroom based on equality. There is a danger when I am the one handing down grades that I can be perceived as the one with the answers and the "right" ideas. I want to teach and model for our kids that their curiosity is just as valued as mine and that they should be creative and take risks with their ideas, yet I decide their grade at the end of the term. Yes—I do write one-page comments at the end of the term, but the grade is what counts for many parents, colleges, and students. Even if I value risk taking in my classes and build it into my assessment, it does not necessarily mean this is true in their other classes.

Burry: I believe that assessment tools should be set up so that the students know what is expected and what levels of effort and performance will yield what results. Armed with this knowledge, students can then determine their own level of performance and participation. . . . [This way] they are not a bottle bobbing on the water, moving at the whim of forces over which they have no control. Instead they learn that . . . the results that they create are directly caused by the choices that they make. Of course part of the bargain must be that the teacher will do what it takes to support the children to attain their goals.

The issue of objectivity in assessment often raises questions about where the locus of authority for assessment should lie. Should all assessment be done in the context of individual classrooms or schools? Is there a role for "external assessments" such as those often mandated by state education agencies?

Chris: My students will be taking a standardized test this spring. The MEAP (Massachusetts Educational Assessment Program) is a test given to students in grades 2, 4, 6, 8, and high school. They are tested in science, language arts, and math. The MEAP uses open-ended questions that students must answer with explanations rather than the traditional multiple-choice, fill-in-the-circle-with-a-number-2-pencil, computer-scored answer. A memo was circulated through our district informing teachers of the impending test. A clear message was sent that we needed to prepare our students for this type of evaluation. Sample questions were sent with the memo, and teachers were encouraged to use these and similar questions in their classrooms. The idea was that we could teach students to take this test.

I have mixed feelings about my school district's reaction to the upcoming MEAP. My immediate reaction is that we should not be teaching to the test. We should be teaching critical-thinking skills that produce young adults who can analyze a given situation and create a practical solution regardless of the form of assessment that will be used to rate their success. This seems like a utopian ideal that is not close to being implemented by the school system or accepted by parents or children. On the other hand . . . what is wrong with having teachers teach to a test if the teachers end up teaching in a way that promotes critical thinking?

The negative effects of standardized, "external" tests—given on one day of the year, often with incredibly high stakes attached—has been well documented in the literature on assessment (Bailey, 1989; Carnevale, Gainer, & Meltzer, 1989; Koretz, Linn, Dunbar, & Shepard, 1991). Arguments opposing such assessments include gender and cultural bias (Brice-Heath, 1983; Hilliard, 1994; Neill, 1989; Sadker & Sadker, 1995), the constraining effects on the curriculum (too much time spent teaching to the test), and teacher deprofessionalization (Boyer, 1983; Darling-Hammond, 1990, 1991; Darling-Hammond & Wise, 1985). Furthermore, teachers often lament the inordinate amount of time spent on preparing for and administering standardized tests; testing is also a considerable item in the educational budget. And yet, for a variety of political and arguably educational reasons, it does not seem that the tests will go away any time soon. If "teaching to the test" does indeed occur, should not the test reflect as much as possible the habits of mind, such as critical thinking, that we value? As Chris suggested, changing the test just might (positively) impact on classroom practice.

Indeed, Duane and Susan reminded us, whichever form of assessment is used, it must be considered in relation to the school, community, district, state, and country. Nor can assessment be separated from curriculum and pedagogy.

Duane: The issue of assessment does not contain itself within the walls of one school site. It overflows from the elementary school to the junior and senior high schools. From there it flows to both colleges and the state department of education. Although a particular school may make some specific and creative choices for their distinct use, eventually its impact will be felt elsewhere.

Susan: We cannot look at any element of reform in isolation. New assessment must be accompanied by new structures. Teachers must be given more time for planning as well as assessment — some of which should happen in conference with students, and some in collaboration with the students' other teachers.

The way that we choose to assess our students both molds and mirrors our beliefs about the act of teaching and the process of learning. To move to "alternative assessments," such as the narrative approach proposed in our role-play, would require fundamental rethinking of the "way we do school." In the end, we decided to schedule another school board meeting. And then we exchanged gifts.

Assessment as Reality Check

HERBERT H. "BURRY" GOWEN II

A young student from East New Rochelle
watched, perplexed, as his G.P.A. fell.
He, when asked to explain
In a metacognitive vein
said, "I dunno. It sure beats me to hell."

Having never engaged in portfolio assessment (though I am really interested in learning more about this), I'll confine myself to the kind of assessment that I have dealt with in my teaching career up to this point. As I have always lived in a grade culture, and will likely return to one, my own personal questioning has usually assumed that the end result of my assessment will be a letter or number grade and a comment for each student. Before the beginning of each school year, I generally like to reexamine some of my basic assumptions about teaching to once again determine if they are in line with my own personal philosophy of teaching. One of the questions that seems to resurface again and again in this ritual reexamination is the question of grades. Can grades be set up to support learning? More simply put, when is it good for a student to get a *B*? For that matter, when is it good for a student to get a *C* or a *D* or an *F*? Put in another way, when is it not good for a student to get an *A*?

I think never. It is never good for a child not to get an *A*.

Had I asked myself this question 6 years ago, my answer would probably have been more mainstream. It was good for students to get a *B* when they deserved a *B*. Only those who did *A* work deserved *A*'s. And we all knew who deserved *A*'s. In a set of expository papers it was easy to spot the *A* students. They were the ones who wrote the papers with the sentences that were more complete, with the better and more sophisticated use of vocabulary, with the insightful logic and flowing argumentation. In a set of math tests it was easy to spot the *A* students. They were the ones who got 100% time and time again. More important, they were the ones who seemed inherently to employ word-problem attack strategies, who almost reflexively checked their tests before passing them in, and who knew how to

68

budget their time during tests. I had been an *A* student for most of my own school career. They were the students like me.

I never felt that I had any problem defending my grade book to parents, students, or colleagues. Usually they agreed with me. We all knew who the *A* students were, who the *B* students were, who the *C* students were, and who the *D* students were. Once in a great while a student would inexplicably rise or fall, but generally people stayed in the same range month in and month out.

In retrospect, I am embarrassed by my smug complacency. I don't think that I was doing a bad job. To the contrary, I had been receiving strong reviews from parents, students, and administrators for my inventive and nontraditional lesson presentations. But in the back of my mind was a nagging dissatisfaction with the whole process. Despite my using storytelling, simulations, role playing, model making, creative writing, crafts, improv theater techniques, and recycled fraternity drinking games, the *A* students stayed *A* students and the *D* students stayed *D* students. I was told that a lot of learning was taking place in my classes. But I wasn't seeing it. Nothing that I tried seemed to matter in the grand scheme of things.

In my second year of teaching, I had an experience that caused me to begin the process of questioning my complacency in all of this. It was parent conference week. It was a cold, gray, drizzly, northwest October day, one of a succession of cold, gray, drizzly, northwest October days that year, and on this particular day I had a conference with Jacob Scott and his mother. Jacob was a chubby, good-natured seventh grader and one of those students you could see was bright but whose work seemed always to be incomplete, half-heartedly attempted, and generally late. His desk was a black hole that sucked in worksheets, and most assignments were turned in as a crumpled ball, usually because he had to fish them out of the bottom of the left pocket of his Lakers jacket, where he had stuck them the night before. No amount of cajoling, heart-to-heart talking, or weekly progress reporting seemed to make a difference. Jacob was a *D* student who on a good day could squeak out a *C+*, and once in a great while a *B−*. Jacob had just gotten a *B+* on a French test, and it was the biggest mistake of his life.

Now his mother was royally pounding on him, as only mothers in conferences, flanked by teachers, can do. She had just finished a litany of his shortcomings and was beginning to pull out guilt. After all of the time they had worked on homework, he still wasn't measuring up. He wasn't organized, he had shown he could do the work, but he was just plain lazy. She was tired of having to go through conferences like this. He knew he was capable of more. After all, hadn't he just shown that he could get a *B+*? How did he expect to go to West Point with grades like this? If he didn't want to be grounded into the next century, he had better shape up and start putting his nose to the grindstone.

When Jacob's mother finally wound down, I asked Jacob what he thought of all this. In a petulant voice, he responded that he thought he was doing OK. This of course set off another blizzard of comment from his mother. For some reason, though, I heard these words in a different way than I had ever heard them before. Where before I had written these words off as a typical middle schooler's pat excuse for laziness and lack of performance, I suddenly heard them as a true statement. Jacob really did think that he was doing OK. He had absolutely no idea of what OK looked like. He knew he wanted to do OK. In fact, he knew he wanted to do excellently. But he was completely clueless as to how to get there.

In a way it was an epiphany for me. I haven't met many students who don't want to do well. I find it hard to believe that there are many kids out there who wouldn't trade sweeping the floors in the stadium for a chance to stand on the victory platform. But I've met a lot of Jacobs, who would love to do well, who expect to do well, but who have no idea what it takes to do well. As a teacher, I now know that it's my job to change that.

It took me a couple of years, some methods courses, and the opportunity to apprentice under a remarkable teacher in Seattle who later became the National Social Studies Teacher of the Year, but eventually I totally redefined what I thought a middle school teacher should be. For me, teaching at the middle school level was as much teaching kids how to learn as it was teaching what to learn. I realized that not every student has the inherent understanding of what it takes to create excellence. Most students that I have met, in fact, don't have the tools to organize themselves, to break down large tasks into manageable chunks, to set realistic and attainable goals, to organize and attack difficult abstract text materials, or to effectively study at home. But that doesn't mean that they can't learn the tools. At least at the middle school level, I decided that study skills were not a part of the curriculum, they *were* the curriculum. I decided that the best service I could do for my students was to teach them how to learn, how to monitor their learning, and how to reflect on the progress of their learning. It was my job to teach my students what it took to succeed, to help them to internalize the process of creating excellence, and then to push them, sometimes kicking and screaming, to go for the golden ring . . . which is where assessment and my earlier comment about *A*'s comes in.

It is never good for a child not to get an *A*.

In saying this, I am not endorsing grade inflation or a lowering of expectations. Quite the contrary, I expect my students to get *A*'s. Or put in more mundane terms, I expect my students to produce excellence. In business, where I cut my teeth before teaching, less than a great job meant no salary raise. It meant that people talked about you on coffee breaks. It meant, at layoff time, that you were the pink-slip color guard for the band heading out the door. The world expects excellence. As it should. As do I.

But high expectations can be a way of holding students in their place. No matter what they do, they can never measure up. Or high expectations can be the spur that propels a student to greatness. I prefer the latter. I like to think of high expectations as a compact between my students and me. In a sense I am telling them that if they walk my road, I will expect nothing less than inspired greatness from them, but if they start down that road, I agree to be right there with them, supporting them, guiding them, and occasionally kicking them in the pants to make sure that they succeed. When they arrive at the first rest stop, I'll be enticing them, titillating them, pushing, shoving, and carrying them, with guilt, excitement, positive feedback, and chocolate-covered peanuts to get back on the road to the next destination. My job as a teacher is to do whatever it takes to push my kids toward an *A* and to give them the tools to reach it.

In this analogy, my assessment strategy plays the part of roadmap and mile marker. Through my assessment tool I lay out for my students what steps they need to take and in what order they need to take them. I try to set grades to levels of production and effort, realizing that some students will require less effort, support, or outside monitoring to get there, and that some will require more. I know that some of my kids write better rough drafts than others. But I will not concede that, by final draft time, my less able learners will not be able to produce a product every bit as good as those students who in my former life would have been *A* students. They just need a more explicit and detailed road plan and the support and feedback to follow the map. When they do produce such a product, the success is addictive.

I strongly believe that a *B* is only useful when it contains a process for the student to make it into an *A*. This is why I have such a disagreement with the concept of holistic scoring, despite the fact that I have used it many times. (Holistic scoring is the practice of using subjective judgment at the end of an assignment to assess a grade, rather than grading based on specific, articulated standards.) I like the implied acknowledgment in holistic scoring that there is a preferred way to approach an assignment. What I hate about holistic scoring is the fact that it gives no constructive feedback to the student and offers no plan of attack for a student to upgrade this or future assignments. In my view, it is an opportunity lost and a waste of time.

While watching the movie *High School II*, I was struck by a comment of one of the teachers who was talking in the faculty meeting at the end of the movie. He said that what he was trying to teach his students was not to abandon a task and say "I can't do this," but rather to stick to a task by saying "I can't do this yet." To me this is the essence of what I am trying to say about assessment. Traditional assessment, given at the end of lessons, units, or the year, acknowledges students who already know what it takes to be academically successful. It does nothing to help or motivate the students who have not yet learned this. When an assessment strategy lays out and rewards the steps to achieving success on an assignment, however, students will be able to buy into the idea that "I can't do it yet, but I will." My assessment strategy can reinforce one of two things. It can reinforce the idea that only the students with inherent ability will be able to succeed. Students without this inherent ability need not even try because nothing will change. Or it can reinforce the idea that everyone, with hard work and effort, will be able to create excellence. The first is a formula that maintains stratification, while the second is a blueprint for accountability and empowerment.

Yes, there are many holes in my philosophy, or at least technical hurdles. How, for example, does one assess interactions in cooperative learning situations? When a task is sufficiently open-ended, how does one assign a judgment to dissimilar approaches or products that, though equally excellent, required vastly different levels of involvement? How does one assess creativity, and what happens when a student makes a good case that the criteria are too restrictive or invalid and then refuses to be bound by them?

These are some of the many questions that I have yet to answer. These are some of the questions that brought me to Harvard. In acknowledging that these questions still exist, though, I have not negated my central precept. Assessment strategies should serve as both a game plan and a reality check for students. Only then can they truly assist students to develop an "owner's manual" for their education.

The New Year

ELEANOR DUCKWORTH

January 10—Potluck

Harvard's fall semester does not end at Christmas. Starting in mid-January there is a period for exams and final papers, and before that is a period of 10 days when some classes continue to meet. The group members were too busy in January to take on planning a session. But we did not like to lose so long a time, so we settled on a working potluck supper in January. There would be no homework, but I would lead a continuation of our assessment topic and a stocktaking discussion.

This turned out to be a good meal, but not a working session. A blizzard that evening turned it into a grand adventure. Not everyone made it. Some had to leave early. Students were preoccupied with finishing work for courses that were ending. We dropped the assessment discussion altogether and ended up making the simplest available decision about our next steps, rather than having a good, sound stocktaking. We decided that I would take on both February sessions.

The first would, finally, get to a discussion of some of the fieldwork; the second would, finally, get back to the assessment discussion. Those "finallys" are intentionally repeated. The year was going by, and at the potluck people were expressing some frustration again about whether we were getting anywhere. I was a little worried.

February 3—Tensions and Resolutions

The fieldwork was the one requirement I had imposed on this seminar (along with a final paper). My guidelines were that each person spend a half-day eight to ten times in a classroom; that they arrange with the teacher some way that the time could be useful—observer, sounding board, co-teacher; and that they arrange to be able to spend at least an hour talking with the teacher each time. In the two cases where a group member was a full-time teacher (Chris and Kris), they became the classroom end of the collaboration—Mark and Doug, respectively, spent time in their rooms.

In this session, three people presented their fieldwork—Duane, Elissa,

73

and Suzy. Essentially, the rest of us listened, engrossed. Suzy's paper, the next Interlude, is the best way to give a sense of their work. This quote from Duane's journal indicates some of the effects on his thinking of having spent time in another teacher's classroom.

> *Duane:* I . . . plan on securing some trained teacher to donate some time to observe in my class. I now see the incredible value in having another set of eyes and ears in my classroom. . . . I realize this may not be an easy individual to find, but I'm committed to seeking them out.

I had reserved some time in the session for our stocktaking, put off from the potluck supper. This turned out to be an important turning point, but that was by no means clear at the time. On the contrary, the journals reveal that people were struggling mightily with this seminar. I started to write a journal at this time myself, thinking it might be important for my own thoughts and feelings about this work to be available to the others. An excerpt from it is included near the beginning of the account of the next (February 17) session, but the comments were written before I knew the intensity of the feelings I had sensed.

> *Suzy:* ETP feels weird to me. So, what's weird? Frustration? Yes. Tense? A little. Dissatisfaction? I couldn't really say that. It is more a feeling of incompleteness than anything else.

> *Jane:* Now in ETP I am faced with a situation so contrary to my former learning experiences that I am continually frustrated and often impatient. Ironically, I am also tangled in a King Midas syndrome. If I could have wished for the perfect way to learn, it would be in a place where the learners are responsible for how that learning happens. Now that I am in that wishful place, I wish it were different. . . .
>
> Our circle has become too circular, for we go round and round too long. Maybe we need to square the circle — either literally or figuratively.

> *Duane:* I was glad Eleanor called on specific people, making sure all spoke, as I have felt robbed of several individuals' insights and thoughts who choose, for whatever reason, to sit in silence.

> *Susan:* I am feeling perplexed because I sincerely am enjoying this whole process, and yet — I can't seem to put my finger on it. . . . What do I even mean by "it"? . . . I believe in student-driven curriculum, but am craving a clearer sense of purpose. In fact, I think that struc-

tures allow and enable students to explore more freely. T-440 was very loose and expansive, and yet very specific, clear, and even narrow in its focus. So . . . maybe we need to work harder at defining our purpose and narrowing our scope. . . .

I have discovered, though, that while working on writing, a group of colleagues can be an incredible source of support and inspiration. I don't see us as "critiquing" each other, but listening, encouraging, and helping each other move our thinking forward. And I believe that just the writing will help us figure out and share what we have to say about our teaching experiences.

Kris: OK, here goes. I'm getting sick of it. I don't want to talk any more about what we are going to write, what we are going to talk about, or any more planning. We need a leader to make these decisions for us so that we can get on to whatever it is we are here to do. That's curious, I don't even know what we are here to do. . . .

For the writing next week, I am going to compile some selections from my journals about my students. . . . It's about time we talked about some real people for a change.

The writing that Susan and Kris refer to had been the subject of most of the discussion. And we did come to a decision. We all agreed to spend half an hour at the beginning of each remaining class helping each other to write.

Doug: I was pleased by the direction taken by some members of the class who were willing to push us forcibly down a path. I was glad the atmosphere was such that I could feel comfortable expressing my displeasure or discomfort with a suggestion (even if I did not get my way).

We chose the following format: We would work in pairs, at first randomly assigned. For 15 minutes each, one person would read to the other, and the other would respond; then we would switch. The writing could be anything—some part of our reflective journal, a paper for another course, a story about teaching, in my case an article I was writing.

That was all there was to it. It proved to be enough.

Reflections on Observing a Teacher

SUZY ORT WITH BETH DONOFRIO

Wonderful things happen in the strangest places. One place where I would not have expected to find great teaching is a "lockup" facility of the juvenile justice system. Then I spent a day with Beth Donofrio,[1] English teacher at a detention center in Boston. As part of a seminar for "experienced teachers," I, a high school social studies teacher, have been observing Beth's class weekly for 3 months. "Watch closely. What do you notice?" was essentially our assignment, a rare opportunity for most classroom teachers.

On my first day in Beth's class, we went to Egypt. Approximately 60 boys, about half of whom were awaiting trial and half of whom had been sentenced for up to 1 year, were issued passports and boarded a jumbo jet for Cairo. Our stewardess greeted each passenger: "Mr. Stewart, how are you? Can I get you anything?" Mr. Stewart responded: "I need a stamp." Reacting immediately, stewardess Beth took out a potato pyramid stamp and obliged him. To a traveler she had never met before, she said: "Welcome aboard. I don't think you were with us last night. What's your name? I'll have to call the embassy and get you a passport."

"My name is John Moore. Can I get a stamp too?" They were playing along! Even new kids fell into the game quickly. Another traveler whispered to the new passenger: "Trust me. It'll be fun. This teacher is crazy." That's a compliment.

Beth is a master of engagement. Educational research tells us that kids "at-risk" (more like "in-risk," I think??) are often too distracted by their problems to focus on school. City kids are too cool to play, too hip to enjoy the world of imagination. Beth disproved all of this. How did she do it? What does it take to engage the "difficult-to-engage" student? I got excited watching her, and I started a list: She used positive reinforcement, encouragement, praise. She made sense of what a student said. She planned a variety of activities. She had multilevel assignments. She radiated enthusiasm. She constantly drew out relevance to students' lives (one funny slip up on this point: during a discussion about the size of pyramid stones that evolved into weights, she asked: "Who can think of something that weighs an ounce?" Raucous laughter. She grinned, only then realizing the drug reference. "I guess I walked into that one, huh?") She made sure there was activity in activities; the activities were also fun. She gave good directions with loud, clear expectations. She had a rich repertoire of attention grabbers as motivational tools—potato stamps, togas, Egyptian feasts, and so on. She paid individual attention to each kid and brought them back when they faded. She also knew her material and what she wanted to teach them. She was confident, she played with them. She knew how to "reprimand" without humiliating or sounding teacherly. Once a kid reported that he got so drunk the night before (in the Egypt role-play) on "champagne on the rocks" that he ended up "asleep on top of a palm tree" and now tour guide Beth responded: "We don't do that here. This is a respectable tour." The kids got it. She had made her point, too. Finally, and most important, she had a trusting relationship with her boys.

Beth's is very exhausting work. Kids space out. Some, it seemed, cannot concentrate; some didn't want to. She tried to engage everyone but also knew when and who to push. "You don't ever really know what's going on in their heads. That kid seems like a live wire—I won't push him as hard as I might someone else." Some kids she didn't even get a chance to know. She had to assess the situation almost immediately and determine how best to handle the kid. Again, this "handling" involved not only discipline. She wanted more than to control them; she wanted to teach them.

In order to teach in this situation, under these circumstances, Beth must have a relationship with each child. *In order to teach.* Not "in order to teach better" or to make it more fun for the kids, but *in order to teach.* In Beth's job there are none of the standby guarantees, the tried and true of the high school teacher. There are no grades. No credits. No nagging parents. No threats to be banned from the basketball team if you don't do what you are supposed to do. Most of the kids have been truant for years. Almost all work well below grade level. Most have failed repeatedly in school and are less than eager to make themselves vulnerable to failure with very little anticipated reward. To take any risk in this environment could be critical; "tough guy" mentality pervaded, and kids feared doing anything that might jeopardize their image. The only surefire motivation in this situation was intrinsic. The kid had to want to do it for no other reason than desire, because he wanted to. "Ganas," as Jaime Escalante would say. I was also drawn to teaching at a "second-chance school" by this honesty, even purity, in the drive to learn. We are there to turn the turned-off students, the discouraged learners, on to the potential beauty of discovery in school.

Beth "teased" out the students' desire, interest, or motivation by trying to know each of them. Personalization. It is no coincidence, I think, that the class she called her "best" is different only in that she meets them twice every day.

Each of Beth's six classes started off with taking attendance. Not uncommon. Beth's roll call lasted a good 5 minutes, though. Precious time in the context of a 40-minute period. She didn't strike me as a teacher who would deliberately waste time. What's going on? As she called the name of each kid she asked, "How are you doing?" Or "How are you feeling?" "How are you?" "Nice haircut." "Is that a new shirt?" "Don't you look handsome today." A question or comment to each kid. Eye contact. They always acknowledged her. Some kids just mumbled a response, but they never ignored her. I noticed that some of the other kids spaced out, look bored, and teetered on the edge of becoming disruptive while this was going on. I asked Beth after class why she did attendance this way. She responded, "I know that some kids get bored or space out when I do attendance, but I like to have contact with each child even if it is only 30 seconds when I call his name." I watched more carefully, and I saw that it also helped her put a face to a name for new kids who might have been brought in the night before and assigned to her class that day. To new students she said, "I don't think that I know you—what's your name?" During this process she also found out who had gone to court, who had been at the nurse or dentist, and finally who had been "locked down" for bad behavior and not allowed to leave his room.

After attendance Beth began class. The first challenge was to focus the students so she could explain the lesson for the day. This typically somewhat onerous task was often further complicated, rather than alleviated (as one might think), by the two guards (called "staff") who must be present in the classroom at all times. It was obvious that they did not respect Beth's efforts to teach the kids, nor did they value the students' attempts to learn. Sometimes it was them, not her students, whom Beth had to ask to be quiet in class. I heard one kid say only half-jokingly to a staff person who seemed to be deliberately (in my eyes) distracting the student from his work, "My parents told me to stay away from people like you." It was pretty funny. The staff people were generally more interested in noise level and posture than in learning. I've heard them call the kids "stupid," "idiot," and "punk" during class. One kid smiled at a staff person who had just walked into the classroom, "How ya doing, Frank?" "Better than you, Nolan." Needless to say, this did not contribute to an atmosphere that is conducive to teaching and learning.

One day, talking over the sound of the staff peoples' voices and an inconveniently ringing telephone (each classroom has one—it was not uncommon for a staff person to talk on the phone in the middle of class),

Beth called the boys to attention. Her "motivation" for this particular lesson involved handing out photographs taken in a previous lesson and using them for review—"What did we see on our trip to Egypt?" "Pyramids," screamed one boy, waving a photograph of him posing under the bright Cairo sun and in front of one of the pyramids of Geza. "King Tut's tomb." "The Cairo Museum." "Nile cruise." The kids got into calling out what they remembered from their "trip," and Beth handed them a questionnaire that asked them to recall and reflect on the unit. By now she had them engaged and they plunged into their questions enthusiastically. The boys worked together often, though she hadn't specifically instructed them to. Beth provided numerous picture books from her town library for them to flip through and to help jog their memories. Again, I was amazed by her ability to engage.

It was not all smooth sailing, however. After the question sheets, Beth asked the students to write some final reflections on their trip in their travelogues. "What did you see? What did you like? What unanswered questions do you have?" she prompted. One student, generally someone who seemed to participate, refused. All the other kids were writing something. Beth went over to him, "Amar, come on. Do a little of that writing. You can write more than one sentence." "No, I can't," he responded. "Come on. Look what you did yesterday." She flipped through his travelogue, where there was indeed a lot written. "What is going on today?" She tried to figure out what was going through the kid's head. "I just don't feel like it." "How can I help you?" "You can't." He wasn't rude. He wasn't disrespectful. He just wouldn't write. "Just one more sentence," she said almost imploringly. I ached with the familiarity of this scenario—that sentence had become very important suddenly. It is hard to pinpoint why. OK. He seemed to be trying. He raised his pencil slowly, half-heartedly. Yes. He's going to do it. I could see Beth's relief. Then Amar dropped his pencil and slumped in his chair. "No."

When I have described this situation and others like it to other people, particularly nonteachers, I often hear, "Well, just make him do it. You are the teacher. Make him do it." If there is one conclusion that I could draw after months of observation in another teacher's classroom and from my own experience, it is that you simply cannot force someone to learn. Beth could have called over one of the guards who had the power to rescind what few privileges the boys have —no TV or Nintendo—and had the kid "locked down" for disobeying. In the face of this direct threat, the kid may indeed have churned out a sentence or two. I wonder, however, if this student would have learned anything from the experience. You can force the sentence, but you cannot force the learning.

Inevitably this belief will be interpreted by some people as "soft" or "do-goody" liberal or coddling. Beth certainly got a lot of this at her school. Unfairly, I think, as she was not afraid to be firm: "Michael, I need to ask you to stop talking. No, I don't want to hear it . . . just say, 'Yes, Beth, I'll do that for you. I'll be quiet.' Thank you." Based on watching her in action and on my own experience, I think more and more that teaching in certain contexts requires a redefinition of some of our long-held views of teachers and students. This does not mean rejection and denial of the existence of any authority on the part of the teacher or structure in the classroom. It does mean that we need to rethink how that authority and structure are expressed and used. When you are in the "business" of turning on the turned-off, the kids who have experienced years of school failure, you have to push steadily, yes, but you have to push gently as well, or you risk losing much more than a single sentence.

For all the accusations of "coddling" and babying the students, Beth is probably the teacher whom the students actually respect the most, behave in the most controlled way for, and consequently learn the most from. After a week-long drama festival that she recently organized, a clinician who sees the boys one-on-one and in group counseling sessions reported that she noted markedly improved behavior on the residence floors long after the end of the school day. Beth's lessons seemed to carry over. She might not get every kid to do everything that she would ideally want him to do. She might get very frustrated and be tempted to fall back on the "just do it" approach, but she knows that ultimately it won't work. Instead, she opts for the gradual change process of showing the kid what is important, why he should do X, Y, or Z of his own volition; thus she models respect and a clear sense of what "doing the right thing" means.

It seems to me that Amar, the student who refused to write the sentence, was having a bad day. This is frustrating for a teacher, but it happens—all the time, it sometimes seems. However, much more difficult to deal with (sometimes because you really sympathize) are situations where a student appears to be just plain mad at school. Once, just after Beth had finished assigning and negotiating kids into reading different characters in *Antigone* ("I want to be Creon." "Can I have a big part today?" "No, I want a big part." "Who wants to be Antigone?") and defusing comments from the guards ("He can't read anyway"), one student who was new to the class said, "Why are we reading this play? Why don't we read a real book? Why don't we read something that will help us once we get out of here?" Beth stopped what she was doing immediately. She turned to the boy and asked very seriously, "What's wrong with this play?"

"I want to know why we are reading," he said, "We all know how to read. We need things that are relevant, that will help us do better on the outside." Beth first tried the approach of "give it a chance before you reject it. Just try it for the period." But he didn't buy it. She then explained that she had chosen *Antigone* because its central theme – the conflict between conscience, on what you believe is right, and what the law tells you to do – is a universal theme and one that is very applicable to life today. He shook his head. No. No. No. Beth knew that the other students were interested in the play. I could see that they were getting anxious listening to this exchange. She asked him again to try for the rest of the period and turned back to the play, hoping that the other students' animated reading and interest would demonstrate how relevant and applicable *Antigone* could be.

The student brings up an interesting dilemma, though. In some ways it is a familiar argument. African American and Latino kids are just not motivated by Greek tragedy. This kid is a living example of that. Blindly imparting "the canon" might not best serve the students at Beth's school; attention should also be paid to "cultural representation," connection, and "relevance."

As I listened to the student, I thought about this argument and I knew that there was something to it. At the same time, I watched the other students, some of whom made *Antigone* relevant themselves – one kid didn't want to try to pronounce "Eteocles" and so read "my man E"; the student who played Creon punctuated the sentry's circumlocutory confession that someone had managed to sneak by the guards and crudely bury Prince Polyneices' body with "Uh-huh, uh-huh, get to the point, man" and nods of his head. These other students were clearly engaged and interested in the story. The post-reading discussion about what "doing the right thing" means and how that depends largely on circumstance also grabbed them. They peppered their comments with their personal experiences and stories. Their conversations led me to believe that the kids were also interested in and connecting to the ideas in the book. It seems to me that by pulling out themes and raising "essential questions," *Antigone* can be made relevant.

At the same time, I think back to the arrival of Nathan McCall's (1994) *Makes Me Wanna Holler* onto the school's scene. This book – the story of a young African American male growing up in a working-class suburb in Virginia who gets involved in street life, gang violence, robbery, assault, and rape before he lands in jail and turns his life around to become a renowned journalist for the *Washington Post* – speaks to the students more directly and poignantly than *Antigone* ever will. Beth bought a copy for one of the kids, and for a few days it lay on her desk. In class after class students would spot the book from across the room, wander up to the desk to look at it and read the back cover. Many asked her if they could borrow it. They had heard of the book and wanted to know what all the fuss was about. I certainly had not heard Beth's students express such interest in a book before.

There is, however, a fine line between "relevance" and material that is interesting to students and believing, in essence, that particular students are not capable of appreciating and understanding a book that is not "theirs." After her teaching day ended, Beth would often go upstairs to the boys' rooms to talk to a student about extra work he might be handing in. One day she went to talk to Tyrone, a boy who had been particularly intrigued by *Makes Me Wanna Holler*. At his own suggestion, he wrote a review of the book for Beth: "This is the kind of book young people, especially black men, need to read more of. There should be more books like this." Upstairs, during the conference, while they were discussing his writing, Tyrone suddenly turned to Beth and said, "I am tired of writing my opinion. I don't want to write about me, my story, or what I think about something anymore. I want to write from another perspective, not only the 'young black male' thing."

I am reminded of a similar incident from my own teaching. One day, at our morning staff meeting, our principal announced that one of our students, a boy who had been in my "American Women" history class, had been shot and killed the night before. Two days later school was canceled so that we could all go to his funeral. The afternoon after the funeral, I found myself unable to plan my lessons. I kept thinking, "What's the point anyway? These kids need someone to listen to them, someone to help them deal with the pain in their lives and with the very real problems—violence, drugs, racism—that they face everyday. I should be helping to become strong, resilient, confident, and good decision makers. Why should I think of an interesting way for my students to learn, remember, and find meaning in the 13 colonies?"

I went to class unprepared, and I told my students that I had been unable to plan a lesson because I was upset about the student's death and that maybe we could just talk about him and how we were dealing with it. After I said this, one kid stood up and said that it was my responsibility as a teacher to teach them something, to teach them "new" things, and to teach them as much as possible because "knowledge is power." I immediately, wrongly and cynically, thought to myself, "Oh, great. I am having an existential crisis, and this kid is not only giving me a hard time but on top of it all, he is spouting clichés at me." But he was totally serious. My students spent the next half-hour explaining why it was important that I continue to teach them subject matter, content. They said that they appreciated our school not only because we gave them an outlet to discuss the things that were going on at home and outside of school in family group (our version of homeroom) but also because we used material in our classes that reflected and complemented their interests without sacrificing the abstract notion of content. They said that often in their other schools they felt that the teachers didn't bother to teach them "content" because they figured that they would never need it anyway. The underlying assumption was that poor kids of color did not need to know the same things about American history as college-bound prepsters did—when are *they* going to use it anyway????

One of my teaching fellows this semester in graduate school shared with me her belief that it is the kind of intellectual abandonment my students were describing that ultimately lies at the root of their cynicism. I agree. I have learned so much from watching Beth challenge the "intellectual abandonment" and negative self-image that many of her (and my) students have internalized.

I underestimated the potential for discovery that this assignment (visit a teacher's classroom weekly) could provide. I have had time to talk to another teacher at length, to carefully observe, and to reflect deeply on such pivotal issues as multicultural education, engagement and motivation, classroom management, and "values clarification" (for lack of a better phrase), just to name a few. After 40 hours of observation and conversation, I am left with a million thoughts whirling in my head. One thought haunts me: After 3 years of year-round teaching at $21,000 without ever having gotten a raise and a new master's degree from Harvard, Beth is going to quit her job at the detention center. How can we hope to raise the standard of education in this country unless we start respecting and appropriately compensating the work of teachers? Another thought encourages me to think concretely: How can we incorporate this kind of extended observation into the professional development and/or preparation of teachers? And finally, inspired and challenged, I think with anticipation about returning to my own classroom.

Note

1. Students' names have been changed. The name of the teacher is unchanged.

A Change of Scenery

KRISTIN NEWTON AND ROSARIO JARAMILLO

February 17

During the week, Kris happened to run into Doug and Susan in Longfellow Hall. They started to talk about ETP. Instead of talking about how great things were and how much they were enjoying it, they found themselves saying things like, "It feels sort of weird." They discussed their feelings that the last class session had been slightly uncomfortable and tense. Those feelings were certainly evident in the journal entries from that session.

Susan suggested that our classroom was not conducive to conversation, that it was too dark and dreary. Though it had windows along one wall, it was below ground level, rarely received any sunlight, and had a few recessed lights that did not do much to brighten the atmosphere. They talked about finding a new place to meet. Kris remembers, "though I was not convinced that changing rooms would help a great deal, I was eager to do anything to address the way I was feeling about class." The three of them went to the administrator in charge of room assignments, found out which rooms were available, scoped them out to make sure they were acceptable, and then officially changed the location of the class. They were amazed at how easy it was! They didn't even need permission from Eleanor, who was not only the instructor but also the leader of the upcoming session.

Meanwhile, Eleanor was making plans of her own and, with Rosario, thinking about this upcoming class.

Eleanor: For some reason, I don't have the sense of urgency that I feel on the part of some in this course, urgency about making sure we get somewhere. That's interesting to me. To some degree, it's not too surprising — I'll be here again; the others won't and want to make sure this experience is everything that it could be while they're here. On the other hand, I do have that sense of urgency throughout T-440. So I think it is something about this seminar, this group of people. . . .

I started thinking about our last two class meetings. At the February 3 meeting, I thought Duane's and Elissa's and Suzy's accounts of their fieldwork placements were wonderful. And it seemed to me that they helped others, who have not yet started, to focus a little on theirs and to think about the potential kinds of value. They also focused my own thoughts, afterwards, on everybody else's fieldwork [placements] and whether people feel a little at loose ends about them. I've been intentionally loose about them. I believe that it is important for teachers to have time in schools when they don't have responsibilities and that they know perfectly well how to learn from that situation. But it's not clear to me now whether my vagueness has made it hard for people to get going. Maybe, on the other hand, simply some time constraints would have been helpful — make sure you've started by December and you've had five visits by March — something like that. (Or maybe in fact everything's fine.)

The other thing I keep rethinking is the amount of writing we should have in this seminar, and what it should be about. Actually, this is related to my wonderings about fieldwork. Sometimes I've tied the writing to the fieldwork. Not doing so this year, writing may have been left too loose, too. I had a thought that the group might want to develop what it wanted to do by way of writing. But I didn't even say that. So I shouldn't have been surprised if nothing came up about writing at all. But I'd have been disappointed and done something different about it next year.

So I felt good about the long discussion about writing together. It's of course still very unclear where it will lead. But I was then (and still am now, even more) very intrigued to see how it will play out.

Afterwards, I realized that this could have been taken as yet another class spent in getting ready to go, and that made me very uneasy. We didn't even get to our discussion of assessment — making two whole classes gone by without getting back to it, when we had all agreed in December that that's what we wanted to do. December! And then I realized that *I* was the one who had taken responsibility for those two classes (one class, one potluck). (The only classes I'd been responsible for since the opening one.) So that's what focused me on relative degrees of urgency.

And then I realized that it was in my ballpark again, a third time. *Then* I did feel some urgency! Get on with the assessment discussion! And get back a sense that we are going somewhere.

Based on the writing discussion in the previous session, and with the above issues in mind, Eleanor gave us the assignment shown in Figure 6.

The room change had been kept secret until the following Thursday, when Doug, Susan, and Kris set up a scavenger hunt that started at the old

FIGURE 6. **Homework Assignment, February 17**

1. Bring a piece of writing and a question about your piece (bring two copies).
2. Bring in an assessment experience/tool from your teaching practice to share.

classroom and led to the new room. There was light coming in through numerous windows, and they pushed all of the tables together to make one large discussion table. Unlike previous sessions, in which one person signed up to bring a small snack that was eaten at a particular time, they spread out a feast of food and drink that welcomed their classmates to the new home.

> *Suzy:* What a great class! I feel a great sense of renewal and more important, positive energy. . . . I feel good because it seemed like there was action taken in the class. People were feeling dissatisfied, and they did something about it. Part of me wishes that we had addressed the "let's change things" feelings directly as a whole group. I like the "get out and air your feelings" model, although it does get oppressive sometimes. . . . One thing that class made me think about was expectation (especially from our assessment discussion) and classroom tone, ethos, atmosphere. This is one of the most fascinating things about teaching for me. How do you as the teacher help create or foster a positive atmosphere in the class? Actually this question reaches way beyond "positive atmosphere" and into something that is difficult for me to describe. I mean the norms, the expectations, the ethos of the classroom. What is acceptable work-wise, behavior-wise, etc.?

> *Jane:* Were we loosened up by food and wine amidst our discussion? Were we simply enjoying the physical nature of a "round table" discussion? The new room and the new seating and food arrangement did wonders for creating a session that was a smoother blend of time and talk.

> *Duane:* I valued meeting around a table. The table has a way of bringing us together and acts as a huge serving tray for both food for thought and food for the body . . . my courses to date here have dealt with teaching and curriculum but little with the physical learning environment. . . .
> While the other room had individual chairs with arm rests/desks attached . . . we sat with a chasm of open space between us that

seemed to create some distance. The table seems to bridge that distance and act as a connector between class members. Ideas offered by members do not fall to the ground but are positioned to be "laid out on the table" for all to ponder and examine.

At times my experience at Harvard, and occasionally in ETP, has been that ideas and thoughts offered for discussion end up on the ground and in that chasm created by this formed circle, and are rarely elevated to an adequate or useful plane for examination. Consequently, the fruits of many individuals' minds go untried and untested and may at times foster a feeling of "why bother" (sharing), stifling individuals in offering their thoughts.

Kris: [What] was helpful to me was finding others who felt the same way I did — and doing something about it. I am not convinced at this point that our feeling of a "new start" is due to the room change, but rather to a determination of someone in the group to do something about the frustration we were feeling. Being able to say "I don't like this" and then actually changing it was very empowering for me. Even if it was only the room.

Susan: I am being struck here by just how complex teaching and learning is. I am reminded of those days in the classroom that felt so disastrous and then those that clicked, and how I couldn't for the life of me figure out what I had done differently — if anything. Sometimes it all feels so elusive — and sincerely determined by some force beyond my control or comprehension. To be honest, I think that part of what I love about teaching is how unpredictable it is and how intuitive it feels. It requires constant assessment, analysis, contemplation, and then action followed by more thought that can lead to the next action. I was really captured by Donald Schön's [1983] notion of the reflective practitioner. The art of teaching does seem to be in our ability to take all of our experiences and apply them in the present to a brand-new, unique situation. And there is nothing like that moment when it all clicks. Those fluid, intense, almost mindless moments are what sustain me through the frustrations and failures. After hitting that one smooth, perfect, popping tennis ball, I am willing to spend hours swinging and slamming shots into the net and over the fence. And I do believe that we learn from those miss-hits.

Jorge: The change of room was not important for me because I [didn't] mind the other one. What made me the happiest was the desire in each one of us to make something out of this course. People were not as introspective and were willing to share their ideas, even if these were not the same as others'. We broke the "confrontation threshold."

As had been planned in our last session, the first half-hour was dedicated to our writing. In pairs, we read our writing to each other so that it could be heard in the writer's voice. Tracey had proposed three questions that she had used in her classes that would help us to listen actively and respond to our partner's reading: What did you hear? What confused you? What do you want to know more about? These questions prompted discussions such that it was difficult to remain true to our half-hour time table.

Elissa: Our session . . . provided an opportunity for me to face writing about some things that have been on my mind in a pretty amorphous way in the past few years. I felt very fortunate to have worked with Susan, who was very supportive and listened carefully to my writing as well as my concerns and fears. I had been wanting to put some thoughts and ideas to paper but never found the time or, I should say, made the time. I even thought of avoiding the issue with our assignment, but in the end I decided it was time to try to articulate my feelings, experiences in teaching during a difficult time in my life. . . .
    The issue of writing and sharing our writing with others brings me to the issue I raised in my last reflection about trust. If we begin to hear each other's writing and help each other with it, it can help us to trust each other more. Or is it that we will grow as writers and listeners when we trust each other more and more? I am not sure yet.

Kris: I had known immediately what I would write about when the assignment was mentioned. It was an opportunity for me to draw from what I had written about my own students, all the frustrations and joys. The things that I wrote meant a great deal to me. Even my difficult students are in my heart, and it was good to talk about them.

Chris: Writing has always been a pleasurable experience for me, although I am not always confident in my skills. The piece that I chose to share had to do with motivation and my eighth-grade student, Dennis, about whom I spoke in ETP during the fall. The piece itself was a little disjointed and needed some work but *it was wonderful* to share the writing with someone who was familiar with some of the things I had said in class but who was not so close to me as to have heard about Dennis all year long. . . .
    I learn about my own teaching and consider educational philosophy best through reflection and writing. This provides specific

thoughts that then can receive feedback. It is direct feedback to a specific thought that takes my thinking to another level. Writing is a very structured way to make sure that my thoughts will be responded to.

Following our half-hour of writing conferences, we divided into two groups to share our assessment experiences in graduate school. The question then was: What might the professor's perspective have been in choosing that kind of assessment? This elicited many different points of view.

This was a shift from our typical seminar: We spoke as students as well as teachers. The group had an honest discussion about our assessment at Harvard. People were open and direct about their views on grades as motivators.

Suzy: Often I think we think that grades are the cues as to what is acceptable and what is not. I don't think that this is necessarily the case. Although grades potentially do set a certain standard, all too many kids are "content" or simply used to getting "bad" or average grades so often that they just accept it. Still others like the Melissas (Sizer's example) just slip by with OK grades and don't really think about what the grades mean (if they actually do mean something in the school). I guess this goes back to our early discussion about reward-free environments. Is it possible to create an atmosphere in the class that seemingly conveys the norms, standards naturally? I mean that everyone or most everyone understands and respects? My experience with Eleanor's class is almost "proof" that it is possible. . . . In T-440 I felt that high effort was expected and to do otherwise wouldn't be enough. I felt this even without the "threat" of grades or consequences. I had another class where I handed in whatever crap I could dish out before the deadline. I didn't really have any of those feelings (maybe a few lingering doubts) that "anything I hand in with my name on it, I should be proud of" . . . because I think that the instructor didn't really care, that whatever I handed in he would accept because it didn't really matter too much to him. Blah! No standards! No rigor!

So I am wondering how to get that "hard work" feeling into my classes. A huge portion of it is demonstrating to the students that you care. That the work is meaningful and important and will be taken seriously. I wonder about the level of student self-directedness and self-confidence necessary for this to work.

Jorge: I heard myself say how important grades were for me. This was partly true. There was an added element of motivation (or pressure?) in the classes where I was graded. However, I hadn't come to terms with how I felt when I found out that lots of the grades (many people had received) were mostly *A*'s. This opened several questions for me. It wasn't a matter of feeling better than the rest, but [rather of] a questioning of the true worth of the *A*. Was my work really worthy of an *A*? Could I have gotten the same *A* with less effort put into my work? In real terms the *A* became a Pass. Both gave me the same information about my work. After being a teacher who gave very few *A*'s to students who did almost perfect work, this system is difficult to understand.

Rosario: Many times external pressures such as grades play an important role in our life as a motivator to do things [the way] the teacher wants them, and yet at the same time [I feel] angry that these things can still influence me, since I find that it takes away so much of my freedom and autonomy and almost of my dignity. I remembered the delight I experienced of not "having to do" anything for T-440 if I didn't want to [since I was auditing the course] and yet doing it for the same reason that everyone else said they had experienced in that class: because we all felt that we were simply learning and we loved it. But then I thought to myself, "having the approval of Eleanor, her recognition, the recognition of anyone in authority, *does* affect me. Is that not the same as a grade?" So why are we trapped between doing things for reasons we don't believe in but that are effective and sometimes not doing them when we don't have the external pressure or the external reward?

Part of the answer came to me in another class thinking about the differences between the *is* and the *ought*. It is true that grades or other external pressures influence us. It is silly to deny that. But *ought* they? What happens when they do? We know our students study more if we press them with grades, but what are they learning when we do this?

Yet the problem with these questions is that they may have a "moralistic" tone. What was nice in our group was how we were all acknowledging how indeed we are affected by these things.

Next we reconvened to share assessment strategies we had used in our classrooms. Burry had brought several examples of student work, and we listened to him explain the assignments and his assessment of them.

Jane: As Burry explained the various kinds of assessment samples he'd brought to class, I began to associate assessment with many different classroom activities. I began to see assessment differently, as a form of evaluation that follows a continuum from informal classroom inter-actions to more serious and planned testing procedures.

Prior to this revelation, assessment meant "test." Now, I realize that when I engage my students (grade 4) in a discussion about all the characteristics of air, I am evaluating their understanding of air. From that point on we might predict certain outcomes pertaining to the prop-erties of air. Again, I am assessing how well they make sense of a par-ticular problem. From there, we will explore and experiment and write about our findings. All the while, evaluation has an implicit role in de-termining how much information the students can assimilate.

Simultaneously, another form of evaluation continues. . . . I am wondering what I could have done differently to improve a lesson, or I reflect about the success of a lesson. I often write comments in teach-er's guides when an idea strikes me as an especially terrific way to teach a concept or when a lesson does not work.

Many teachers (myself included) dislike nonteaching duties such as "yard duty." As I think about greeting the students as they arrive in the morning, it is easy to spot a child who did not have as cheerful a morning as we imagine young children to have. Here, again, is a form of assessment. If the child is in my own class, I can assess his or her state of mind and offer some additional support as he or she enters the classroom. I guess the evaluative continuum begins as we enter the school each day and continues until we leave in the P.M. On second thought, does it ever end? Thanks, Burry, for opening my eyes.

Chris: There is one assessment topic I wanted to discuss that was only alluded to: Standardized assessment is an important issue that is being reviewed at many levels and is currently undergoing a lot of change. As teachers, we each are faced with students having to take standard-ized tests. Questions of preparation and objectives arise whenever I think about this type of assessment. If we are leaning toward changing our teaching styles to become more student-inquiry-based, we must look deeper into how we will know what these students have learned. We must also realize that the teacher is not the only authority evaluat-ing students. States each have an assessment plan, and the most com-mon plans include some form of standardized tests.

I have heard teachers say that when they "allow" students to learn in a more exploratory manner, their students will not be well prepared for the standardized tests. This speaks volumes about what we value as teachers. It seems to me that these values are somewhat different from those of people who make the standardized tests and of the indi-viduals who mandate that school districts give the test to their students. If the values were the same, there would be less of a question of how students would fare on the test. The test would measure what is valued by all parties — the teachers, the test creator, and the school administrations.

Before the closing circle, the group made some decisions. The first was that we would continue to bring in writing to share with a partner at the beginning of each class. The second was an informal agreement to meet during the off-weeks. This idea was something that had been brought up several times during the first semester. The responses ranged from those wanting to have a formal class every week to those not wanting or not able to meet in the off-week. On this particular night, when the mood of the group was so positive, there was a strong desire not to lose momentum. We agreed that those who could would meet for dinner and conversation the following Thursday at a restaurant in Harvard Square. It was the start of something new. A 3-hour class was not enough. We had more questions and ideas to share than 3 hours every other week would allow. We valued listening to each other and having experienced teachers listen to us. We were realizing that we were truly becoming a caring and committed group.

Eleanor: I wonder if it was other people feeling somewhat the same way that prompted the efforts to create an atmosphere of renewal in the last class. Maybe. In any event, I thought that atmosphere was terrific.

What was important to me about the assessment discussion — what was important in my thinking about it ahead of time — was that it was to be an occasion to talk about our own experiences as teachers and to learn from each other's thinking — something we all want to do and which we have done very little. So I was eager to get that going; and I hope we'll keep planning for it.

And then Kris's responses to the last class [February 3] also focused me on trying to find ways for people to talk about the struggles.

And I did feel good about this class. It did feel as if we are on our way again.

Now I think that it's very healthy that someone else is planning again. I really appreciated the variety that resulted in the fall from having different people do each class.

Three Events Important to Humankind, or Something to Drop

CHRISTOPHER WHITBECK

March 3

> If you give students conflicting interpretations, they get to use their big, bright brains. . . . Have faith in the students' ability to think. . . . Learning [comes] not just in memorizing facts, but in mastering the skills of thinking as well as critical attitudes. (Bateman, 1990, p. 10)

Last week's class worked. Kris and I decided we wanted to use the momentum. We sought to push the group to a new level without a lot of group process. Eleanor thought we were planning too much, but we knew how we wanted to approach an issue that was important to Kris and me.

One of the greatest pleasures of the ETP seminar had been to rethink ideas that we had come to believe we understood. Many nights we experienced confusion — mental discomfort caused by discussions or activities that presented facts which conflicted with our previously held ideas. This evening we wanted to formally investigate methods that could be used to bring these feelings about. What happens when the teacher is no longer a giver of knowledge but instead elicits questions from students and creates experiences that challenge prior beliefs? This was modeled in T-440; some people have referred to it as "constructivist education" or "teaching through exploration."

During our planning session we divided the class into two groups, science and history. The two groups received differerent homework assignments (see Figure 7). We planned to break into two separate groups and then return for a whole-class discussion. We also wanted to leave time to discuss the goals and directions for our weekly writing conferences.

During the previous semester, Kris and I had designed an investigation of the physics of falling objects. We wanted to find out how kids developed their understanding of falling objects and had worked with Kris's high school students as well as my middle school students. We knew that kids had strong reactions; they became excited and enthusiastic when the teacher

FIGURE 7. Homework Assignment, March 3

We have decided to address the topic of student-centered learning and understanding students' understanding. We feel that they are interconnected through a method of teaching that we will call teaching through exploration, which we define below:

Teaching through exploration—Giving students time to investigate a subject, develop ideas, and discuss those ideas as a way to learn more about what students are thinking, in order to help students come to a greater understanding of the subject that they are studying.

Your Assignment:
I. Consider the definition given above and the following questions:
    1.   How have you taught through exploration in the past?
    2.   Would you want to teach in this way more in the future? How could you do that?
    3.   What problems have you run into in the past, or what challenges do you foresee in the future, with regard to teaching through exploration?

Feel free to bring examples of things that you have done in the past to share with the group, but understand that those who did not share during the last session will be asked to share their experiences first.

II. Readings:
Perkins, David, & Blythe, Tina. (February 1994). Putting understanding up
    front. *Educational Leadership*, pp. 4–7
Bateman, Walter. (1990). *Open to question: The art of teaching and learning
    by inquiry.* San Francisco: Jossey-Bass. (pp. 3–35).

III. Groups:
1. <u>History</u>: Please bring to class the dates of three events that have been
    important to humankind
2. <u>Science</u>: Please bring to class three unbreakable objects

was no longer giving answers. We had similar success with a group of adults in our T-440 section. We believed that the experience would stimulate a powerful discussion among the adults in the ETP science group. Kris brought several objects to class: Ping-Pong and tennis balls, a feather, a golf tee, a box of tooth picks, and books. Our classmates brought different types of paper, dollar bills, credit cards, and aluminum foil. The question

Kris used to facilitate this group was, "What do you notice about how these things drop?"

> *Rosario:* I truly understood what it means to enjoy learning in the sense that we were really laughing and having a ball in the "falling objects" group, and at the same time understanding through the experience what it meant to understand. . . . It was loose and free, yet focused and precise. We were left to wonder further, to discover more things with the strong notion that we could figure out things ourselves without having to turn to ready-made answers that exist in books and the scientist's mind.

> *Tracey:* I was totally intrigued trying to figure out why things fell the way that they did, and when I returned to the room, I was very curious about all the dates on the board. . . . That session was a continuation of something that has been happening more frequently for me in our sessions — collecting ideas for my own classroom. I have been taking notes during our discussions about what we have done and what others have described, and I really feel like I am gathering ideas for the future.

> *Kris:* I have done some work, as we all have, this year on the topic of student understanding. I feel like I am really learning more about how to work with students to get them thinking. . . . There are so many aspects of physics that come up when people watch the way that different things fall through the air. I like being able to share something that I helped develop. I plan to use the falling bodies as a unit in my freshman classes next year. Every time I work with it, I learn more about how people understand gravity and air resistance.

The question for the history group was, "How would you organize the important historical events that you brought to class with you?" This question had evolved from the November 18 planning discussion. Rosario had explained that when she was teaching history she had students use an index card file for organizing important dates. While we were sharing stories about never understanding the connections among historic events, Eleanor had pointed out that Harvard graduates in 1636, the year that Harvard was founded, could not have had music by Bach at their graduation. She had been amazed by this realization: "How could there be Harvard without Bach?!" This led to an idea of developing multiple-level timelines to study the connections between historical events. We did not discuss how many timelines would be used or what each line might represent. That could be left to the students; the entire process could be an interesting learning experience.

We decided to see how our classmates would construct their understanding of the connections among historical events collected by the group. As per their assignment (see Figure 7), the students assigned to the history group brought with them a list of dates and events that they thought were important in history. The events ranged from the birth and death of Christ to the fall of the Berlin Wall. Eleanor, Kris, and I decided to begin the activity by hanging paper with three blank lines on the wall of the class-room. I had intended the lines to represent categories of human experience (political, social, religious, etc.) but left it to the group to decide what the lines would represent. We each added dates to the three lines, one person at a time, until all of our dates were represented on the three lines. It was difficult to discern how the group members organized the lines. The activity prompted a powerful discussion.

> *Duane:* It was revealing to see what events each individual highlighted. As we constructed our timeline of history I was struck by several thoughts. . . . Thursday's activity reminded me that omissions are in-herent; and we are biased by our experience and perspective. It was noteworthy that (1) there was only one non-Western event listed; (2) there were no events listed between Christ's death and the year 1000; and (3) there seemed to be a weightedness in our timeline toward the modern era. These were not surprises but rather reinforced what I have long felt about my (and perhaps others' as well) instruction in his-tory.

> *Jorge:* Listening to other people's dates, and why they had brought them . . . gave me a better idea of how my classmates think. It made me understand them better, made me see what was important for them. . . . Chris asked us, "Where do we go from here?" At first I didn't know. Now I see these [three timelines] as a great history pro-gram. A class could study history focusing on individuals, [then] coun-tries, and ending up with global situations. An analysis could even be made by seasons. Heck, this could be a good research topic . . . a year's work laid out in 35 minutes. Not bad!

> *Suzy:* I certainly didn't mean to sound negative about the history activ-ity — I enjoyed the activity and have been thinking about how to use it my class next year. I am unclear, however, on its "exploratory" na-ture. Perhaps I am getting too wrapped up in semantics, in what ex-ploratory means. . . . "Exploratory" evokes "experiential" or "doing"

to me. I want my students to make history, to get into it, to play, to experiment with it like they might with falling objects. Fieldtrips, especially in a city like New York, help, as do neighborhood, community research, ethnographic projects; but that doesn't help get at that ominous body of "traditional historical knowledge."

It was a pleasure to try something about which Kris and I both felt passionately. We were working with a pedagogy that both of us had used in our public school classes. We also had learned from the experience of facilitating last term how to structure time for the group and what they might enjoy. On the other hand, we found ourselves wondering if we were being too selfish with the class time. The activity and discussion were very helpful to us, but were they as helpful to others? Were we serving the interests of the whole class or just ourselves? The journals helped us answer that question.

Jorge: In some schools, teaching for understanding may not go over well. As I mentioned in class, my idea, and I think the idea of many people in Colombia, is that teaching is explaining. Many people — not only teachers but students, parents, and administrators — will not understand this new methodology. They are going to think that the job is not well done. I have to be careful how I introduce this when I go back. Perhaps I should not introduce it at first. I should wait; teach traditionally at first, and when I have more confidence, start changing . . . see what results come up.

Jane: I have long believed that children need to "do" what they are learning instead of trying to understand concepts from a textbook alone. I loved the history activity. It gave the historical events a life that they would not have had laying in a textbook. I wish we had more time to debate the issue of purpose. I feel teachers need to unveil their purposes in the classroom; otherwise it seems like we're playing a game, like we're holding back, a secret of sorts. Purposes are meant to be open, revealed, not something the students try to guess. A purpose holds a lesson together; it is like a loose thread, not one that constricts, but one that allows for flow in different directions. Just as our group has been grappling with our own purpose, so do students need at least a general reason for their own learning.

Kris: I continue to wonder why is it so difficult to get teenagers to wonder? . . . There were many more questions associated with this topic that came up in our discussion.

1. How are high school students different from adults? Why is it so much more difficult to engage high school students in activities such as falling bodies?
2. Do students understand the point of open-ended activities? How can we make the purpose of the activity clear? Is it necessary that the student fully understand the purpose of every activity?
3. How do you develop an entry point, a hook for an activity? Is it necessary for the entry point to be connected to the purpose of the activity? If there is a hook for the students, do they need to know the purpose or will they explore just to explore?
4. What makes an activity explorative? Can history be explorative?
5. How do you assess an open-ended activity?

Chris: What will it take to make my students more excited by the prospect of finding things out. I'm describing the idea of learning for learning's sake. Whenever I bring up this question I feel as though I am being extremely idealistic. Some would say that students in their adolescence are uninterested in learning at all. They are a raging tempest of hormones who are lucky to make it through the day without exploding. Middle school teachers should be teaching these students self-control and organization. Build the basic skills and let the high school teachers worry about creating the knowledge. . . .

I think the problem is that in most of their educational experience, the answer was valued. The process was not important. Considering and evaluating other explanations was never done. Get the right answer, get it fast, and get done. Free time to the group that finishes first. My students are much more interactive during free time. They share ideas and debate. I want class time to be free time — a free time to figure things out. A free time to be excited by debating other ideas and experiencing the pleasure of finding things out.

Following the discussion of our falling objects and history activities, we took some time to share concerns about our weekly writing conferences. Focus was a problem. What do I write about? To whom am I writing? Does my writing make sense? Because we were in a class, we thought that we should be doing some writing. So we wrote. Some were very focused; they would work on their final writing assignment. Others didn't know why they were writing. But still, everyone wrote.

Rosario: With our writing project I have mixed emotions: I don't have things written in English that I could bring to class apart from things that I am doing here in classes. But I'm not sure that I have the time or the interest in the effort of writing in English about something I don't even know what to write about.

I liked reading Susan's essay, although I was a bit lost at the beginning. I kept wondering why I was missing the main point. I actually felt rather slow and dumb and that made me even slower in understanding the reading, but when I finally got there I was very interested in what she was pursuing. Perhaps my difficulties began with the fact that it never occurred either to Susan or myself that I didn't have the context to understand the reading. Since it didn't have a title or an introduction, I was trying to figure out while she kept advancing. Also, the educational setting that she was describing was quite different from those I am used to, and so I was creating the context in my mind and trying to picture the atmosphere she created in the classroom while, simultaneously, trying to get a feeling of the impact she was trying to convey to me as a reader. . . . Finally I got the courage to say I wanted to go over it again and reread it and was glad because I finally managed to get involved in a way that allowed me to get deeply into what she was talking about.

I tell these personal feelings for two reasons. First, because I feel that expressing them is important because I like the way that people talk about their frustrations and emotions in our group and want to be more a part of that situation. Second, and perhaps more important, because I want you (whoever is reading this) to know that part of my not understanding has a lot to do with cultural contexts: When you are faced with a new setting, it takes time to understand what is going on. You feel out of synch and out of "harmony" with the other person, which at least to me, makes me feel insecure. And the more insecure, the more out of synch. That makes you seem slow, and perhaps unconcerned, when actually what is happening is that you are adapting to a lot of new situations.

Kris: I like the idea of creating a piece of writing for an outsider, as a product at the end of the course, but I am unsure what shape that final piece will take. I am not sure where my current writings are leading, and I am getting anxious about beginning work on something that will lead to a final product.

On the way home from class, Chris and I talked about our final writing pieces. His idea was that we bind all of our writings together at the end of class as a collection of reflections about teaching. I really liked that idea.

The Search for Wonder:
A Continuing Mission

KRISTIN NEWTON

Kris found a shape for her writing piece. She raises questions about the problems facing teachers as they encourage wonder in their classrooms.

This is a story of my search for wonder in my students over the course of a school year. It is about my coming to understand wonder and the kinds of things that make the world a fascinating place. It is also about my learning to listen to my students and trying to help them find their wonder.

Throughout this year at Harvard, I loved listening to Duane talk about his first and second graders, their questions, and their sense of wonder. The way his eyes lit up when he talked about his students reminded me how wonderful it is to teach children who are full of curiosity. The greatest joy of teaching is having students ask questions like: "Why does it do that, Ms. Newton?" "How does that work, Ms. Newton?" The urgency in the students' voices expresses a true desire to know and understand. It is the wonder that accompanies such questions that helps to get me through the late nights, endless grading, and numerous bureaucratic hoops that go along with the job of teaching. I want more of my students to experience that kind of wonder about science and their surrounding world.

There are few people who exemplify that type of wonder. The realization that wonder seemed so rare in my students and peers caused me to analyze further the situations in which wonder has been exhibited. This year I have been struck by three examples in particular.

I realized early in the year that Seth was a very special student. Not only did he have an intuitive sense about physics, but he also loved to create scenarios and ponder the physical ramifications of such a situation. As a student in one of my advanced physics sections, Seth began to wonder about absolutely everything. It was as though the world was a huge puzzle for him to solve. It was a wonderful challenge to teach him because he missed nothing and never stopped thinking. He also asked incredibly difficult questions and didn't give up until he had a satisfactory answer.

On many occasions Seth has stayed after class to ask me about things that were confusing to him. Right now the thing that he is wondering about is how a magnetic field can continually exert a force on something without violating the law of conservation of energy. This is related to a question he has been pondering since December, when we began talking about gravitational fields. I haven't given him an answer to his question, but he keeps thinking about it and incorporating new ideas into his question.

Eric is a student in one of my sections of Introductory Physical Science — Basic, a ninth-grade required science class. Eric wonders. Recently, we were practicing answering sample open-ended questions from the Massachusetts Educational Assessment Program test to start preparing the freshmen early. We had been asked to do this by our department head. One of the questions was: "The moon orbits the earth. Explain why the moon doesn't fall to the earth." This is a pretty complex question for freshmen, but we jumped in. The freshmen had some crazy ideas about the moon, gravity, and space in general. They also had a lot of questions. For their homework assignment, I asked them to think more about the moon and write down their ideas. Eric raised his hand and asked, "Are you going to tell us, if we don't figure it out?" He seemed convinced that it was beyond his ability to figure it out, but willing to try. I promised to try to explain the next day.

The next day, I brought in some objects to use to demonstrate orbital motion, and I started being a bit more directive and correcting some of their misconceptions about gravity. Most of the students were completely stumped by the question. It was getting close to the end of the period, and we hadn't quite figured it out yet. Eric said, "Ms. Newton, you said you would tell us the answer. You said you would tell us how it works." I agreed and tried to regain the attention of the class. Then I heard Eric, "Hey guys, be quiet! She's going to tell us. Be quiet, or she won't have time." That's not the first time that Eric has expressed that kind of desire to know, and it certainly was not the last.

Rachel is an English teacher and was also in my T-440 (Teaching and Learning) section last fall. Rachel wonders as well. The example that comes to mind is related to an activity that Chris Whitbeck and I did with our section one night in December (and also with the ETP group during the March 3 session). We presented many materials to the participants, and they were to experiment with the way that those materials fell. We did not give any answers or tell any one person whether or not their theories were correct. At the end of the session, several people wanted us to explain the behavior of falling bodies, and some did not want to hear an explanation. Rachel was one of those who did not want to be told the answers, so she and few others left the room. They wanted to figure more out on their own before knowing any answers.

During our January 4 class session, almost a month later, Rachel grabbed me so that she could tell me about the discoveries she had made. She had continued to think about falling bodies in the time since we had done our activity, and her thoughts had led her to some insights about floating and sinking. She was very excited about her conclusions, and she had reached a point where she wanted to know if they were right. They were, and I told her so. I was amazed and impressed by her enthusiasm. She had continued to think about the problem so that she could resolve it in her mind, and then she had taken her conclusions and applied them to a different situation—if only everyone could experience that kind of excitement!

Those examples inspired me to begin to think very carefully about wonder and what is special about people who wonder or the situations in which they wonder. I was hoping I could learn more about what it would take to get the rest of my students to wonder. Too many of them seem to have lost their wonder as they have grown into teenagers and adults. Something about aging seems to cause this devastating change in the way that students look at the world as they leave their elementary school years. I wanted to find a way to bring back to life my students' wonder and fascination. My questions and concerns became a mission that was inspired by the Seths, Erics, and Rachels of the world.

My mission led me to examine my freshmen classes more closely. I was curious about the difference between my students in the ninth-grade physical science course and the students in my advanced physics classes. What was it about my upper-level students that helped to bring out their curiosity? Would my freshmen be like that when they became juniors and seniors? Would they ever wonder the way my physics kids sometimes did? The answers were a little frightening to think about. I wanted to convince myself that they could wonder and become curious again.

In that spirit of looking for a topic with wonder potential, I began developing a chemistry unit based on fire. We started by burning different objects and determining what factors were necessary in order for something to catch on fire and then moved on to fire extinguishers and how they work. The specifics of what is happening when something burns led to a more general discussion of reactions such as combustion and what causes certain things to react chemically with each other. That is where the Synthesis of Zinc Chloride lab came in.

I found myself wondering at the end of the "zinc lab" if it had been worth the trouble. We had taken a day to go over the procedure involved and the safety issues, two days to carry out the reaction and measurements, and a day to review the lab. After all that, I don't think that most of the students understood the major point of the lab — that compounds are formed in certain ratios, regardless of how much of the individual elements are used. On the whole I found myself discouraged, until I realized that there had been so much more involved than just the constant ratio concept.

Some of the students were fascinated by the mere process of doing the lab. In a nutshell the procedure was as follows: Zinc metal was dissolved in hydrochloric acid, which released hydrogen gas. The zinc combined with the chlorine in the acid to form zinc chloride, which was then separated from the remaining water by evaporation. As the zinc began to bubble away on the first day of the lab, I got questions like, "Why is it doing that? What is the smoke that is coming off? How long will that keep bubbling?" On the second day the lab consisted mainly of watching the liquid boil away. I considered the process fairly mundane, but they watched, some very intently. Their interest was not in the ratios and calculations, but in the fire, the liquid, and the acid.

One instance stands out in my mind as particularly interesting. During the evaporating process, I attempted to get Denise, Nikeysha, and Kevin involved without straying too far from the groups and the flames. It proved to be impossible. For reasons beyond my understanding, they have stopped doing any work, and for the most part they refuse to participate. One of the students, Kevin, is by far the brightest student in the class. Not only does he refuse to do any work, he attempts to disrupt other people and gain attention. His lack of commitment and interest has been a serious concern for me since early winter.

Toward the end of the period, after the solid had been evaporated out of the solution and massed, Kevin came over to me and pointed at the working groups, "What are they doing, Ms. Newton?" I explained the reaction that had taken place and the evaporation. He listened carefully. I asked if he would like to see the first part of the reaction, the zinc dissolving in acid, since he had been in in-house suspension the previous day. He said that he would, so I asked him to help me set up the test tube with the zinc pieces. He then poured in the acid and watched, asking why the test tube had been placed in a beaker of water below. I explained that the reaction created heat and that the water in the beaker cooled down the test tube. He looked skeptical, so I took out the test tube and handed it to him so that he could feel it starting to get warm. By that point other students were crowding around and wanted to observe the reaction as well. They passed the test tube around and then placed it back into the clamp. The students left a few seconds later as the music played (our version of "the bell").

I was amazed by Kevin's question. I had not solicited his question; rather he had come up to me and asked quietly and sincerely about the experiment. Kevin had been difficult and noncommunicative throughout the period, and the change in his attitude had been fascinating. I wondered what had caused it and if it were re-creatable.

All of the experimenting with topics helped me to see that my freshmen do wonder and they have lots of questions. The experimenting also helped me to realize that they had been wondering all along, but I hadn't been looking. I didn't think they cared, so I didn't see it. In planning my lessons on fire, I attempted to find out what the students were thinking, and in many cases I found out that they had questions and curiosities.

These realizations led me to believe that all my students wonder but many of them keep that fact hidden and private. It isn't very cool to wonder and have a desire to learn. This became clear to me during our Honor's Assembly last Friday. I was pleasantly surprised to hear Eric called up to accept an honor roll certificate, especially since there were very few boys among the 25 freshmen who received honors. Later in the ceremony he was also honored as one of 13 students out of the 400 in our program who had shown significant improvement during the third quarter. After the ceremony I looked for him so that I could congratulate him. I was very proud of his efforts, which I had noticed in my class. When I located him, he was goofing off a bit with his friends, and they were joking about his awards, asking him if he thought he was smart now that he had the certificates. Their jibes made me sad and helped me to understand how difficult it must be for students to admit that they care and wonder.

It must also be a bit frightening for students to realize that there are so many things they don't understand. In a world in which teenagers feel that they have little control, the search for knowledge is very likely not exciting and challenging, but rather very threatening. In large, public classroom situations, students refrain from voicing their questions due to a lack of self-confidence. That silence is easy to mistake for lack of interest and motivation. It isn't until the students are pulled into a small-group situation, or have the opportunity to talk one-on-one with a teacher, that their questions come out, tentatively at first, more quickly after a bit of encouragement.

I don't by any means intend to imply that this is a simple or universally applicable process. There isn't even exactly a *process*. It's just a realization of a need to change my attitude toward my students. I have come to believe that deep inside, students have the desire and capability to wonder, but that often that desire is hidden or suppressed. Maybe, after gaining the students' trust, finding an appropriate hook, and eliciting a question, more of them will admit and share their ignorance.

The incident that I described about Kevin was very powerful for me. The attitude I had been sensing from him and other students in the class was very defeating for me. Every day I faced the impossible situation of engaging students who knew that they had already failed the class for the year. I was beginning to give up on them. For me, his question was a very important victory, not because Kevin was changed in any way, but because his question changed me and the way that I perceived him. I learned from him how important it is to listen and respond to questions. That may be at the heart of the issue. If we strive to find out more about our students, to listen to them and really try to understand them, they will begin to believe that we really care. They might begin to trust us enough to reveal to us a little bit of ignorance. They might trust us enough to wonder.

Thursday Night at the Movies

JANE KAYS

March 17

Susan: It is so curious to me that just last semester the same 3 hours could feel so cramped and rushed, while now they feel relaxed and expansive. We seem to move more slowly and yet get so much more done. I am reminded of just how important a sense of community is for enhancing learning. I can see my classroom at the beginning of the semester when everyone is stiff and awkward, and the learning process is stiff and awkward. By the end — when it is impossible to recall how the beginning felt — we are settled into being with each other, the classes flow, and the time can feel so much fuller.

It is mid-March, and there is evidence that the group is beginning to feel like a community. We are beginning to challenge each other's ideas and to even disagree, all the while maintaining a sense of collegiality. As Susan's reflection implies, this session did feel fuller, and maybe even overflowing, with enthusiasm and ideas about teacher roles. Doug and Jorge, the facilitators, filled this evening with imaginative teaching strategies that flooded our minds with the many varied implications of how we think about our roles in the classroom. One week prior, they had given us a reading assignment (see Figure 8).

During the first part of the session, we formed two groups. Each group watched segments of a different movie about a teacher. After the viewing, we were asked to decide whether we, as members of a school board, would grant tenure to the educator in the film.

One group watched 10 minutes of *Dead Poets Society*. In this segment, John Keating (played by Robin Williams), the new English teacher in an all-boys boarding school, challenges his students to think for themselves. "You must constantly look at things in a different way; just when you think you know something, you have to look at it in another way. Strive to find your own voice." At this point, John Keating encourages each boy to stand on his desk and look at what lies below from a different view. Keating's approach is often unconventional and sometimes a novelty to the boys, who

FIGURE 8. Homework Assignment, March 17

We will be investigating the different roles teachers play in the classroom. We do not intend to discuss the different jobs you might be hired to do within your school or school system. Instead we would like you to think about the variety of ways you imagine yourself within your classroom setting. We hope that there will be a wide range of feeling on this issue.

Please read the enclosed articles before class:
      Escalante & Dirmann (1990)
      Hill (1994)

We apologize for the length, but we have tried to prepare materials far enough in advance to ensure that you have time to enjoy the articles.

have not been exposed to such unorthodox techniques. However, he seems to confuse challenging with chiding. One wonders whether he is reaching out to his students or targeting them. A poignant example unfolds in class when he berates a student, Mr. Anderson: "Are you man or amoeba? Don't think I don't know this assignment scares the hell out of you!" Mr. Keating has just told the class that he expects each boy to write a poem and recite it in class. Mr. Anderson is withdrawn and is expected to follow in the footsteps of a successful older brother who had attended the same school. It is obvious that the student is uncomfortable with the assignment as well as the class.

The other group watched part of *The Paper Chase*. Professor Kingsfield (played by John Houseman), in his intimidating manner, calls upon a new law student on the first day of class. "Fill this room with your intelligence," he bellows. He admonishes Mr. Hart for not knowing that the assignment for the first day of class was posted and states his expectations for this rigorous course at Harvard Law School. "I call on you—questioning and answering—I train your mind. You come in with a skull full of mush and you leave thinking like a lawyer." Humiliated and nauseous, Mr. Hart races from the lecture hall to the nearest restroom.

Watching these films set the stage for a different and lively format as we shared our contrasting opinions about each teacher's ability to fulfill our expectations of excellence. Each group debated the question of respect and the use of scare tactics in the classroom. Is it our role to weed out those who may not fulfill our highest expectations? What about those students who do not perform as well as other students but love the subject? Finally, in class discussions, how do we handle students who have not done their work? And how do we differentiate them from people who are simply shy?

Duane: "Thursday night at the movies" was an enjoyable experience. Watching *Dead Poets Society* brought back memories of when I first saw the film. I remember being quite moved by the passion with which Robin Williams's character taught his students. Yet this time, years later, I saw him in a different light, and his image did not have the brightness it had before.

In viewing the film Thursday night, I saw a man, a teacher, passionate in the role he played, but much more a performer than a facilitator of his students' learning. And I wasn't convinced that he knew *where* his impassioned performance was leading his students.

I've reflected on why the change in my view of the teacher since I first saw the film years ago. Has my perspective on teaching changed since then due to my own teaching experience? Has it changed due to what I've experienced and learned at Harvard this year (including ETP)? Or did it change because I was asked to view the film through the eyes of a board member entrusted with the task of determining whether the teacher should be rehired? My belief is that it was probably influenced by all three.

Tracey: Our session last week has left me with many questions about teachers. I was fascinated by my wish to accept Robin Williams/Mr. Keating on some sort of gut level — I really wanted to like him as a teacher. Yet, when it came to specific characteristics of his teaching, I liked him considerably less.

Burry: One of the ways I judge the success of a class is the amount of time I spend thinking about the class after I leave. . . . Our most recent class is no exception to this. On my way home and for the next several days, I debated with myself whether I would have renewed Professor Kingsfield's contract.

Rosario: I also enjoyed the movie [*The Paper Chase*] and found the discussion that followed it very interesting because we had opposing views. For some the teacher [Professor Kingsfield] was self-serving and very disrespectful of his students. For others, he was being hard in order to liberate them from their cultural, familial, and school ties; his harshness was understood by his students and fully appreciated. But was he really liberating them, asked someone, or just turning them into his own image? . . . Some people transformed and reshaped their

initial ideas, others kept tightly to them, but we all understood that
the task of deciding whether to give our once-revered hero tenure implied considering the many tensions between ideal and real roles of the
teacher.

Eleanor: Last night I got some new thoughts about teaching T-440 —
about getting different voices into the classroom. Taking a cue from
Mr. Paper Chase!

I found myself saying that I thought it was fair enough for him to
expect people to have done the reading and to be able to say something about it if called on. Then we got into a good discussion about a
number of things. One was how to respond to someone who hasn't
[done the reading]. If you're perfectly nice to them, then there's no reason for anyone to care whether they haven't done it. That was one
view. I don't think I agree with that one. I think people mind being
caught out like that, and this discomfort is reason enough. If they
hold the teacher in any esteem, I think this is the case.

Another was sorting out how to be particularly nice to people
who are reluctant to talk not because they haven't done the reading (or
were daydreaming during the demonstration, or whatever) but because
they're shy, or simply hate talking before a group, or are sure they
have nothing of interest to say. On this last point, I think it's critical
that the question they are asked be one about which anybody who's
done what all the students are supposed to have done will have something to say. I do try to make my questions that way already (infinite
variations on the "say one thing you noticed" theme, for starters). And
while I phrase them that way so that any shy person would feel they
had something to say, no shy person ever has to, because there are
more than enough nonshy people to fill in the time available. I think I
could ask the same kind of question, but call on people. That could be
made clear from the outset, that that's what to expect. And then, at
least at the beginning of a discussion, we could get to hear a variety of
voices. As the discussion proceeds, and people want to comment on
each other's thoughts, nonshy people would again dominate, I imagine. Although maybe I could think of something else for this part.

Chris: The people in my group were discussing Professor Kingsfield as
he berated and intimidated students into learning law. Mark said that
this was the world that lawyers faced and that Kingsfield was an acceptable teacher because he was preparing these students to become
lawyers. In this context he was OK. The students had to learn to accept treatment like this, and if they couldn't, they shouldn't be law-

yers. Kingsfield was part of the process of weeding out those who shouldn't be lawyers.

Having gone to a university where professors believed that they were there to weed out those who did not belong in the sciences, I strongly disagree with this role of the teacher. . . . I took classes where the average exam grade was 18%. If you received an 18% or better, you got a *C* on the test. You misunderstood or did not know 82% of the information that the professor had taught, but you were still an average student. But if you got *C*'s, you were not going to medical school. The professors knew this and performed a service for the university—they weeded out students. Their service should have been to teach the students.

After our discussions in the two groups, we used a "merry-go-round" format to tell each other about our separate viewing experiences. This exercise was another example of an effective teaching strategy that can be used when groups need to share experiences with each other. We sat facing each other in concentric circles, the inner circle having seen one film and the outer circle having seen the other. The outer circle rotated their seating every 2 minutes, and each new pair shared the time, each person answering a question about the teacher in the film he or she saw. The questions had been determined ahead of time by Doug and Jorge, for example: What decision did your group make about whether to offer the teacher tenure? What was your personal view of (Mr. Keating or Professor Kingsfield)?

Rosario: The "double wheel" way of telling what had happened in each group was very neat and enjoyable, far more powerful than having someone making a summary. The diversity could be maintained without overextending in time, and everyone had a chance to speak and be heard. It also made us be brief, concise, and precise.

We had been to the movies and had shared our opinions about the fictitious roles the teachers played. The preceding activities stirred our thoughts. We now moved into the main work of the evening. We entered this segment with lots of enthusiasm and lots to say about the many roles we played in our classrooms. The class blossomed with a brainstorming session that generated a long list of terms to describe our roles as teachers. Some of us offered explanations about the terms. Sometimes we needed to put the role into a context, and other times we had to define some of the newly formed word/phrases. Our list seemed endless (see Figure 9).

When the chalkboard was full, our facilitators asked us to work in pairs to select the two roles we felt were most important. Amid much

FIGURE 9. Teacher's Roles

adviser	helper	mentor	philosopher
grader	clown	evaluator	social worker
librarian	enforcer	weeder	tour guide
friend	assessor	judge	disciplinarian
tyrant	exciter	secretary	baby-sitter
guide	listener	critic	god/goddess evaluator
reifier	reader	nurse	housekeeper
humorist	warden	chaperone	encyclopedia
scholar	reformer	learner	electrician
janitor	mediator	confessor	role model
peer	protector	peacemaker	entertainer
priest	detective	thinker	mother/father
explorer	lecturer	researcher	group-builder
coach	counselor	cheerleader	nutritionist
doctor	liberator	encourager	community-builder
reflector	facilitator	sharer	inspirational-knowledge/builder

protest, Doug and Jorge compromised. Instead, we prioritized five roles. Even this task was difficult. There were so many terms from which to choose and so many seemed important. The six pairs developed the following lists:

1. Detective, liberator, scholar, exciter, community-builder
2. Mentor, listener, explorer, assessor, helper
3. Philosopher, encourager, coach, listener, learner
4. Listener, mentor, counselor, inspirational-knowledge/builder, sharer
5. Mentor, reflector, humorist, facilitator, scholar
6. Adviser, learner, listener, liberator, explorer

Many of us see ourselves as listeners and learners. However, our discussion of the terms revealed that we also had different interpretations of similar roles. For some, listeners are those who listen to their students. For others, they are those who listen to themselves as they reflect on their practice. Our list reveals how differently we see ourselves. The following reflections reveal how much this session influenced our thoughts about teacher roles.

> *Chris:* Teaching roles so often remind me of the paperwork, mediation, and custodial jobs that accompany teaching. A discussion of these roles so often leads to a gripe session. Everyone sits around and says, "How do they expect us to teach when we have all these other things that we are required to do?" I did not look forward to another session like that. This is exactly why I was so pleased—instead of griping, we tried to identify those roles that embody a good teacher.

> *Elissa:* When I started teaching, I had no idea how much I would be asked and expected to do. I also had little idea of what roles I would take on. . . . I am struck by the parenting I do inside and outside the classroom—as a teacher and adviser and coach. I value the work, but it's daunting, the authority kids give us and that we could take on if we wish.
>
> One of the words we put on the board was *coach*. I realize how much I am a coach both on the field and in the classroom. This is a role I feel comfortable with because it allows the listening, the guiding, the modeling, the sharing of the experience with the students. And the fun!
>
> Among the other words I felt tied to were *explorer* and *listener* and *learner*. Especially from my last 2 years of teaching and from my experience at Harvard (especially in T-440). I am more connected to these words than ever before.

> *Jane:* I realize that when I am in the classroom I do more than guide my students' learning, but the last session crystallized my thoughts on the many roles I really assume as teacher. From moment to moment our role changes. We acquiesce according to the cues we receive from our students and become the mediator or the humorist or whatever the moment requires. We continually throw off one hat for another as if in a one-man show.

> *Suzy:* This is an issue that I (we) profoundly struggle with at University Heights. Where do you draw the line? The kids are desperately needy and surprisingly willing to open up. One "trick" teachers used to get kids engaged was to develop a relationship with them. Often this relationship entails becoming a student's confidante. We also have 1

hour per day that we called "family group" devoted to nothing in particular — and everything — self-esteem building, health, sex education, ethics, complaints about your teachers, sharing, extra tutoring, and on and on. I came to see family group as the most essential element of the school. I had 15 to 23 students (the number fluctuated as I would "lose" kids), and they were mine until they graduated or left the school. I used to call six of them in the mornings to wake them up for school. I spoke to their parents or guardians pretty much once a week. I called home every time a kid was absent from school.

Tracey: We make incredible demands of teachers (and therefore, ourselves). We expect them to have attributes that will allow them to plan intelligent, engaging lessons. We expect them to explore alongside students, bringing them to higher and deeper levels of understanding. We also expect them to be good listeners/coaches/mentors/advisers. The final words we chose encompassed, in some way, nearly all of those originally on the board. How reasonable is this? After 3 years, the effort and mental energy required to plan a week's worth of lessons still drain me. Then I have to teach those lessons and respond to the resulting student products. In addition, our ETP group also feels I need to advise my students, listen to them, become individually involved on a deep level. While I would dearly love to be and do all of those things, I truly don't know how long I would last. I don't think I was doing all of those things last year, or, at least, not consistently or all at the same time.

Chris: It was especially eye-opening to me when we identified Jaime Escalante as embodying all the roles that we thought were important for a teacher, and yet we saw this as kind of scary. Yes, Mr. Escalante is a powerful educator with great motivation skills, but I shared Mark's feeling that I wouldn't want him as a teacher. I think he is too intense. . . . There are some [qualities] that I admire: being straight with my students, giving the highest-quality materials, being a nutritionist, and even, to some level, having an open line of contact with the home (although I doubt I would ever tell a parent they must stop drinking because it interferes with their child's science learning). The idea of ganas (a Spanish word meaning "having a desire to achieve") is wonderful. I want my students to have ganas. But it seems to me that Mr. Escalante's students all have ganas by the time they get to him these days.

Doug: I wrestled in my mind how we should end class. As the discussion was winding down, a question continued to occur to me that I

wanted to pose to the class, not for discussion but for individual con-
sideration. For fear of creating tension and frustration from an undis-
cussed topic and from a desire to promote closure, I stuck to a more
traditional approach. In retrospect, I wish that I had posited my question. So I will do so now, having edited that question following suggestions from classmates: What should be the top priority for a teacher?
His or her students or his or her own life? Or can/should these two
realms be considered separately?

Reaching Out and Letting Go

ELISSA WOLF

This paper addresses a question about how teachers prioritize personal matters in their lives and whether they can or should separate these matters from school issues. When a serious personal matter arises, do we inform our students? How do we decide what is best? Elissa's story offers one alternative.

I was never so touched by my students as I was in the fall of 1990. We were sitting in my classroom, room 8. I was 1 among 18 of us sitting at the square table, which is the centerpiece of the room. Some looked concerned, some seemed curious, others seemed off in their own world. I felt anxiety in the pit in my stomach, and I could feel my tear ducts opening. My heart was racing. I was suddenly unsure of how I was going to tell them my terrifying secret. I started to talk. I do not remember my first words, but I do know my voice was on the verge of cracking. I offered a few sentences and phrases, and then I said the words: "I have Hodgkins disease . . . it's a form of cancer."

I had said it, and I could feel myself holding back the tears. And as I looked around the room I saw stunned, saddened, and scared expressions. One of my field hockey players dropped her head; another student looked out the window. There was a heavy silence that seemed to last for a while. I continued to explain the more optimistic side of my recovery. Most of them knew that I had already survived Hodgkins disease once before, during the prior spring. I had taken a leave of absence, and I had not had the opportunity to tell them face to face of my illness since I had been diagnosed over spring vacation.

So, here we were together in my classroom looking forward to discussing the Renaissance in Italy but instead it was a discussion on the rebirth of my illness. I wanted to reassure them (and myself) that I was going to have a full recovery. I told them that I was going to teach part-time and coach through the end of the fall season. It was important to offer them time to ask me questions. I think they appreciated my openness and honesty, as I did theirs. After responding to questions of who would teach my classes, what kind of treatment I would have, and host of others, they wished me well. Several students stayed after class to give me a hug and offer support. It was then, in talking with this small group, that I broke down in tears. To have these teenagers reveal to me that they were very sad and very scared was both a wonderful and a terrifying thing. There I was trying to be a role model of strength and courage and also one of honest emotion. But somehow it was all real. I offered them my fears as well as my strength. In exchange for my honesty, I received overwhelming support and understanding from many.

I had close relationships with some of my students, and these were at the root of my being able to be open with them and they with me. Joan was a senior whom I had coached and taught; we also enjoyed each other's sense of humor. Joan stopped by my classroom one day during lunch. It was a week after my first chemotherapy treatment, and I had lost my hair and was beginning to lose some weight. She casually expressed concern about my not eating lunch and insisted that good nutrition was at the heart of my recovery. I told her that I had been trying to eat well (as I always had), but I did not have a strong appetite that day. We then chatted a few minutes about the upcoming field hockey tournament, and she left for class. The next day, on my desk, I found a lunch bag filled with pasta salad, an apple, and a can of juice. I had never felt so moved by a meal in my life.

It was through this offering that Joan and I began spending part of lunchtime together. She would surprise me each day with a healthful lunch. However, many times I thanked her and told her I did not want her to go to all that trouble; she persisted. I was, of course, very touched by this effort and kindness of hers. Joan was an independent and mature senior who did not often show signs that she cared about many people around her, at least those at school. When she continued to bring me lunch, I could only think that she was a caring and thoughtful young woman who perhaps felt a little sorry for her teacher. It was not until I reflected upon this experience as a whole that I considered that this was not only an act of love but also a way for Joan to give. She was from a privileged family and was often in the position of receiving. Now, at the age of 18, she made the choice to give and share her generous spirit with someone. I was very lucky to have Joan bring me meals and support. Perhaps she was fortunate to know that she brought happiness into my life every day simply by showing that she cared enough to act on her feelings.

Although I was depressed and worried many times throughout my illness, I was very thankful that people like Joan came into my life in a more profound way. I contemplate why it was not only Joan but also other students — many students — who reached out to me in a variety of ways. Had I not been so straightforward and honest with them about my disease and how I was feeling, I wonder if I would have lost an incredible opportunity for support and they would have lost a chance to show the understanding and warmth of which they are so capable. Had I protected them and myself from embarrassment or fear of rejection, I feel sure that my year would have been far more depressing, more alienating, and more frightening.

My school and my students were wonderful gifts because they were there every day. Each weekday when I woke up I knew that students would be waiting (perhaps not always thrilled by the 8:20 hour of our literature class) for class to begin and for a chance to talk about the works we were reading and the ideas we had. I had something to look forward to each day. Whether it was an interesting discussion or a presentation by students or just spending time with other people whom I could connect with, my school community helped me along every day. Importantly, they helped me to define myself not just as a cancer patient. Through them, I could see that I was also still a teacher.

Honesty was central. As I mentioned, I was forthright in discussing my illness. As the weeks progressed, my physical appearance changed (I lost all my hair and became more pale). I had thought about wearing a wig, but it felt uncomfortable and I thought it looked unnatural. I decided to wear colorful bandannas and scarves and would often wear a fun hat in the winter. Students would compliment me on the scarves and ask where I had bought them. During the year, several students and faculty members brought me others to add to my growing collection. When anyone at school asked about the treatment, I told them about it. I thought it was important for me to be as real as I could despite the circumstances. Outside my school community, people would occasionally stare at my head in a scarf. My students simply did not do this, or if they did, they did not ever let me see them doing it. I thank them for that; they treated me with dignity and respect and would not be put off by my physical differences.

Of course, as a teacher, I still considered myself a role model for my students. Although aware that I was nowhere near perfect (before, during, or after the illness), I still believed I had some qualities and experiences that were important to model and share. In addition to being honest with them, I wanted them to see and understand that a sense of humor was key to my recovery and could be an antidote to struggle or challenge. I had brought humor into the classroom before my illness, and I continued to do so. For students to see someone still laughing and perceiving the humor in life while undergoing a tough treatment and disease must have been significant to them. I was being me in my class. Except for the obvious physical changes, I was being the same teacher who loved what she did, who was trying to improve her craft, and who enjoyed a good laugh.

Besides the profound and terrifying reality of my own mortality, I was also fearful of losing my job. I was beginning to love teaching; it was bringing more and more joy and challenge into my life. Having been a teacher for only 2 years, I was learning at a fast rate and was eager to continue on this path. The school support was incredible. I was offered the opportunity to work part-time and complete my season of field hockey coaching. My school could not have been more caring and supportive. The administration put no pressure on me to push myself more than I could; I was to do what was best for me. Several weeks into my treatment, I became ill and missed 2 days of school. Upon my return, I was informed that my fellow faculty members had offered their sick leave to me if it was ever necessary. Again, I was shown only love and empathy. Rather than simply feeling sorry for me, my colleagues reached out and took action to alleviate my anxiety. I continue to be very grateful to them.

Although I did not need to make use of their sick days, I was "sick" twice a month. My chemotherapy was scheduled on Monday afternoons of the first and second weeks of the month. This would allow me to teach that Monday and miss the Tuesday following the treatment. It did not seem fair to me or my students to arrive in class overtired and ill at ease. At first I was very concerned about missing too many school days and this being unfair to my students. It was not that I thought they could not live a day without me; rather, I did not want a lack of consistency due to my missing too many days to get in the way of their learning.

After several months of missing 2 days a month, I began to notice a change in my students. They began to take greater charge of their own learning. I was very impressed with them. They knew I would not be there on certain days, and they became even more responsible for their own work and class time. I would tell them the plan the day before, and I can honestly say they never let me down. They did not always get as much out of the class as I would have liked, but in all honesty this happens when I am there, too!

The same thing happened with my field hockey team. I had to leave school a couple of times because I was feeling quite ill, and my seniors ran practice. I would leave a plan and discuss it with them. That year we were second in the state tournament. It became even more clear to me that coaching also involved letting go of authority and trusting your kids. I did this both on the field and in the classroom, and my students rose to the occasion and made us all proud.

There are many ways in which my illness has informed my teaching, and these examples are evidence of why. In my second year of teaching I slowly began to let go of the complete responsibility for making kids learn. I tried to help them see that it was mostly up to them and that I was there to guide them in this journey. It was not until I was ill that I fully realized the meaning and impact of this. Students will learn if they want to. Obviously it is important for a teacher to provide the environment and a few interesting ideas. I am confident that my students learned as much, if not more, the year that I missed school twice a month. They learned about wonderful literature, and they also began to understand what it means to be a responsible learner. They realized that if they did not take charge of themselves in class, little would get done and they would lose out. It's striking that an illness can force not only the patient but also those around her to grow and challenge themselves.

Upon my return the following fall, 3 months after my last treatment, I felt that some profound changes had taken place within me and, therefore, within my teaching. As I mentioned, I confronted much more clearly the issue of authority in the classroom. Whereas I gave more responsibility to my students when I was ill because of my physical absences, it was now becoming an important part of my teaching philosophy. From the first day of classes, I informed my students that they played the major role in their own learning process. I was clear in stating that I was there to help keep things interesting and even to clarify issues but that the important learning would come from them as individuals and as a group. I can say with confidence that my teaching has been improving a great deal as I embrace this philosophy. The more responsibility I give to my students and the more trust I have in them, the more they seem to do and the more leaps they take. I had always based my classes on discussion, but now this has taken on a new meaning. What we call "student-centered" teaching has emerged from my newfound ideology. If my students have questions, I expect one of their peers to help them with their understanding. I rarely lecture or "give" them information. I always expect them to come ready to engage themselves with questions and ideas in our discussions or group work.

This process has been very successful, and I know there are other factors involved. I work with a caring, supportive, and educated parent community. I do not walk through metal detectors to get to my classroom, and I have had few discipline problems in my classes. (There are few in the school, for that matter.) I realize I have worked with some very bright and motivated students. In addition, I am quite aware that European history is not the be-all and end-all for most teenagers. It is not what they talk about late at night at parties. I am not foolish enough to think that my class is the most important thing in their lives. But what I do believe is that because I have been touched by a fearful illness and because this experience allowed me to reach out to my students, they have taken steps to becoming more mature and trustworthy and responsible in their own education and in how they conduct their own lives.

In the end, the most important thing is that I was honest with my students and that I expected the same integrity from them. As we got to know each other and trust ourselves, we learned together and I became a better teacher. I still have difficult memories left from this illness, but I am convinced that I could not have had as enlightening and healing a journey as I did without the supportive company of my students.

An Extra Teacher's Mind

KRISTIN NEWTON

March 24

In an earlier session, Eleanor had described our fieldwork requirement. Specific fieldwork experiences ranged from working in an after-school program to observing particular students in a kindergarten class. Some people completed their fieldwork during the fall term, but most worked on their projects throughout the spring. Some members felt unclear about what they were doing. Many were eager to share their experiences and receive feedback from the group.

Because of Harvard's spring break, we had decided to meet 2 weeks in a row rather than miss 2 weeks in a row. However, that meant meeting the night before spring break began, when Elissa and Mark would not be present. It was very rare for a member of the group to be absent, and, as Duane noted, we "missed Elissa and Mark's presence and input." This provided a second reason not to address a "bowl" topic but rather to have Eleanor and Rosario facilitate a discussion of our fieldwork experiences.

Members were to describe their fieldwork briefly to the whole class. Mark and Chris were working together in Chris's middle school science classroom. Mark videotaped class sessions, and the two of them reviewed the tapes to see how students interacted during group inquiry. Jane was working with a kindergarten teacher, observing and discussing three children about whom the teacher had concerns. Burry was observing classes in a Catholic middle school. Jorge was collaborating with teachers in an after-school art program. Tracey was collaborating with a high school teacher in a school that was using 97-minute periods. This teacher was using the longer blocks of time to engage her students in a project consisting of improving the school library.

Next we split into two smaller groups to discuss two situations in detail, so that the group could think together about what can be learned when an extra teacher's mind is available in a classroom. The two situations were chosen because the participants involved had questions about their role in the classroom and wanted the opportunity to discuss their situation with a group of people. Susan's work with a history teacher and Doug's work in my classroom were the focus of the resulting small group discussions.

Eleanor: I was glad Susan picked up, earlier in the evening, on my asking who'd like some help thinking about their fieldwork. She pointed out that she didn't want to feel she *needed* help more than anyone else. Her point was right on, and I so often forget to say that part. I like to focus on one person's work as a way to get closer to the issues that are at the heart of *everybody's* work.

Susan wanted to understand better her role in her work with a history teacher at an alternative urban school. She wondered what to look for and how the issues and questions would emerge. She believed that the direction should evolve organically through discussions with the teacher, but she worried that without any defined agenda, nothing would be accomplished. Doug was observing my ninth-grade science classes, and we wondered if he should be actively involved with the students or be more like the silent observer that Susan describes below.

Susan: The more time I spend observing other teachers, the more I am daunted by what it takes to be a great teacher.

I appreciated the time people spent this week consulting with me about my fieldwork. It definitely helped me to recall my purpose and to clarify how to take advantage of this time. . . .

I do believe that humanities can be taught "through exploration," as Chris tagged it [during the March 3 session], but it does feel elusive at times. I am just thinking that one tip is to slow way down. One teacher I am observing tends to set a fast pace and to keep them interested through his excitement. I myself was definitely swept away by the infinite amount of interesting information there is to learn. His knowledge made me so hungry for more. Perhaps, however, at times it is important to give students that opportunity to delve deeply. I will never forget spending 4 hours drawing a picture of Plato's cave [as part of a final project for T-440].

I sincerely hope that I can keep this inquisitive, focused, critical stance when back in my own classroom. I think this approach is one of the most valuable lessons I am taking away with me from this year.

Kris: Doug and I certainly appreciated the advice from the people in our small group regarding his role in my classroom. Based on the advice from the group, we are meeting more often to discuss my freshmen classes particularly. We have talked specifically about my lessons and how they worked in class. Doug has begun to take a more active role in the class.

I have really enjoyed having someone observe my class whom I trust. . . . I was very nervous about having another experienced teacher observe me, which happened last fall, when Doug visited my class for the first time. I was worried that he wouldn't think that I was doing a good job. That didn't happen. When we have discussed what happened in a class, we talked about ways to attack some of the problems that come up day after day in my freshmen classes. I have gotten many new ideas, but mostly it is reassuring to talk to someone realistically about what works and doesn't work. It's nice to hear someone say, "Yeah, they really are difficult kids."

Doug: Kris and I immediately put the discussions to work by discussing her plans for the next day, reforming some ideas and leaving the rest the same. I also decided to make a conscious effort to become more involved in class.

The next day was a great success. The students were interested in Kris's discussion, they enjoyed the exercise on measuring the speed of wind-up toys, and they were surprised when the class was over. In the second period, I encouraged one of the students to challenge Kris to a contest (we had previously agreed on this idea). He thought it was a great notion, and the entire class became involved in the challenge — who (including Kris and me) could, using limited resources, protect an egg from breaking when dropped from the second floor.

Because several people had had questions about the purpose of the writing pieces we had been sharing in class, we ended with a discussion about our final paper requirement and how that might relate to the writing pieces. Eleanor and Rosario presented a few options for our final paper and invited other ideas. Options included writing about the fieldwork experience, writing about a previous teaching experience, and reflecting on the year by referring to the journal entries that had been written after each session.

During our discussion of the final papers, it turned out that several members of the group, independently, had considered combining our writings into a book. Much discussion followed. Many people were intrigued by the idea of publishing, although there were concerns about how such a book might be organized. Some people in the group were not sure that they wanted to write a piece for publication. Others did not think that the paper they planned to write would be appropriate for such a book.

Duane: As I have sat and listened each week to different individuals' written thoughts and reflections, I have been impressed by people's giftedness in expressing themselves through writing. I think the possibilities for a collaborative collection of experienced teachers' writings are endless for our group.

Doug: I cannot say that I have been transformed into an avid and eager writer by this year of study. . . . If I had actually done what was assigned, I would now have nine different volumes of my own reflections about my studies and teaching.

Tracey: I wonder about the next step: Exactly what do we do now? I have been putting off working on my piece because I now look at it in a different way and am not sure if that will affect my writing, let alone whether that would be a good or a bad thing.

Eleanor: I was happy with the way the class went. (On the other hand, I have a feeling that at this point we can count on classes going well — everyone will make sure that they do!)

I think the book is a fine idea. It was neat that it seemed like a straightforward and do-able idea to everybody — with so little hassle. (Of course it remains to be *done*.)

Can the Community
Be Our Classroom?

Susan McCray

April 7

Some of the most rewarding time of ETP was spent in conversations outside scheduled hours. Through such talks, Rosario and I had discovered a fascination with each other's work. We had a common interest in enhancing academic learning through spending time with the community. Each of us had experienced the rewards of developing "real-life" experiences for young people, and each of us was intimately aware of the complexities and questions embedded in this pedagogy. How do you ensure that time spent out of the classroom is integrated into academic learning? How do you prevent service learning from becoming forced volunteerism or just helping for a day? How can teachers pull this off without adding hours of extra work? In planning this session together about the community as classroom, we hoped to spark excitement and to grapple with the issues. For homework, people were asked to read a chapter by Freire (1985) and a description of the program in the school where I worked (McCray, 1993).

Although our sessions were limited to 3 hours, Rosario and I decided it was crucial for us as a group to experience rather than just discuss this topic, so we planned a mini-exploration. In designing the session, we struggled with many of the issues common to this curriculum. Considering our time constraints, we wondered how directive to be. Should the group develop its own plan and driving questions, or should we do it for them? We shared a strong philosophical belief that students should be involved in creating their own investigations but wondered how we could practically accomplish anything (in 1 hour) without structuring it ourselves. While fearful that people would be frustrated by so little time, that they would not come up with any ideas, that they would be bored, that they would make a joke of it all, we decided to trust the process.

Before going out, we opened the session by asking the group to generate questions and to brainstorm different ways in which the community could be a part of schooling. Our list ranged from engaging students in exploration of a given content to preparing them for the job market. We discussed the definitions and effects of service learning, of social activism, and of citizenship, as well as the importance of connecting with parents and other community members. On the surface, we were discussing the definition of community, but it soon became clear that once again we were analyzing the purpose of education and the role of the teacher.

Elissa: Whether it is community in our classroom or school or both combined, I believe that developing community is essential to a good education. If one of our educational goals is to help foster "good citizens" or caring and responsible humans, then I think we must engage in the process of developing community and working with the one around us.

Jane: Because I do not live in the community where my students live, it is important that I put myself out there, to interlock "me" with "them" and mesh our differences, in a way that fosters an appreciation of each other. When I took my class to the senior citizens' center, I felt that there were three communities fusing—seniors, children, and the white teacher. In a small way, each of us came to know each other a little better. I feel it is important to look at service learning as an "ask not what I can do for you, but what you can do for me." . . . To see it as a "helper/helped" endeavor is to marginalize one participant at the expense of the other. Rather, service learning is a way to grow—each of us. It is a way to expand our view of the outside world and bring it closer.

Jorge: I was somewhat doubtful about this topic. I couldn't relate to it very well. But the way it was presented and the exploratory activity made it one of the best classes for me. Another aspect of teaching was presented to me, and also a new tool.

At the beginning of the meeting, I suggested that we define the term *community*. I thought it could be used in two ways, with regard to the outside community (e.g., neighborhood) or referring to the building of personal relationships within the group. It seemed clear that everyone was thinking about the former concept, so I didn't insist.

Now I will insist. I felt the importance of building classroom community in the curriculum that Susan had us read for homework. This is especially important if one is responsible for a group of children. The relationships among the children affect their academic and emotional development. So these activities outside the classroom also have great importance for this other reason.

After the short opening discussion, it was time for our exploration; we divided the class into small groups based on the grade levels and disciplines that we teach. The goals were simple yet challenging to accomplish. We asked each group to choose an issue related to its discipline that could be addressed through exploring the community and to develop a strategy for studying it. We charged each group with interviewing at least one person and bringing back at least one artifact that represented part of their journey and what they had discovered. And then, we were on our way.

In that short hour, each group had a rich and unique experience. The elementary teachers—Duane, Jane, Jorge, and Eleanor—walked out of our classroom unsure of where to go and what to do. They decided to head toward the Repertory Theater, thinking it might have programs for young children. Unsure of how to begin, they looked at the photographs in the lobby and read the fliers about current productions. (They brought one back as their artifact.) A woman who looked as if she belonged drew their attention, and they risked trying to interview her. They lucked out: Her first response was, "I teach clown." After explaining the place of this theater skill, she took them into the theater, where a rehearsal was in progress. All in all, the visit opened their eyes to the many educational possibilities offered on both sides of the footlights.

With the same enthusiasm, the math and science team—Kris, Burry, and Chris—developed a very different experience. They saw the potential in the city for authentic research and experimentation; before even leaving our classroom, they had developed a full scientific study. Once ready, they worked their way to a local brew-pub, where they studied how beer is made. They brainstormed hypotheses, gathered data by sampling beer and interviewing the waiter, and drew conclusions. As with the first group, the sense of fun seemed only to enhance the learning. They took a topic that interested them and created an academic experience—without its seeming academic.

The other two groups were made up of humanities teachers, and by coincidence they all ended up in the graveyard together. Doug, Tracey, and Rosario went to find out how old the graveyard was and to search the tombstones for clues and insights into the past. They wondered what you could learn from reading tombstones. Doug, a Latin teacher, found many stones engraved in Latin, which he imagined his students translating. (They brought back a rubbing as their artifact.) They discovered the infinite number of paths into history.

Elissa, Mark, and Susan, while also in the graveyard, approached the

experience from yet another angle. Before going out they talked a long time
about possible interdisciplinary studies. They discussed a variety of themes
and guiding questions about life and death, generational changes, and religion. They had hoped to incorporate some form of service or community
action into their curriculum but didn't know where to begin. Once they were
out, before even entering the graveyard, they wandered into the church and
found a soup kitchen. It seemed too easy; all you have to do is look and
there are ways to help. They were reminded that the only way to find how
to help is to look for yourself. While walking back to class, they generated
a variety of curricular plans for connecting work at the soup kitchen with
studying history, the graveyard, and the community.

When groups returned excited, we wondered whether the enthusiasm
came from developing their own ideas, the actual discoveries, the freedom
to wander, or all of the above. Often we propel our students into exploration because of the potential for the unexpected.

Duane: I remember walking down Appian Way on our way to the theater wondering what, if much, we would find there. I remember walking up Appian Way on our return to class wondering where to begin
our report. The possibilities for learning were seemingly limitless in
that brick-and-glass building not even a block away.

When we returned to class, it was great not only to share our discoveries but to hear of the other groups' discoveries. It was as if Columbus, Balboa, De Soto, and Margaret Mead had all come together
to share what their discoveries had revealed to them. "Oh, yeah, well I
learned that . . . " It was enjoyable to hear how one group made beer
tasting an authentic scientific study. (It gave me an idea for a second-
grade science project comparing low-fat, whole, and chocolate milk.)
And then to hear how the groups took two very different learning
paths from the stillness of a colonial graveyard reinforced for me that
there is life after death.

Eleanor: I was astonished that in an hour we had such a great field-
trip. (A good deal less than an hour, in fact.) Somehow I felt guilty
the whole time that we weren't really trying to figure out how we
would use such a site with kids. But it was a wonderful visit for us.
Kindled my own fascination with theater again.

Elissa: I can't wait to get back to teaching next year; I hope I have people around me who want to engage in conversations like the one
Mark, Susan, and I had. . . . In deciding to go to the graveyard and
explore some things there, we met someone who told us about the

soup kitchen and how they help feed the homeless and poor. It is difficult to articulate the feeling I had, but it was really something to be "out there" looking for one thing and finding another. I look forward to making a much stronger effort to take advantage of my community next year in the hopes of building one within.

Tracey: As I was walking to the Ed School from Harvard Yard the other day, I stopped by the graveyard to read the signs along the fence. My group's activity had really made an impact in that my curiosity lasted. This is a goal we should have for students — that their learning continues after the lesson is over.

While we all felt the energy from "getting out," the activity raised many questions about the feasibility of integrating these kinds of experiences into academic instruction. Concerns included the logistics of planning and supervising experiences for large groups of students, as well as ensuring student engagement and academic development. We are all aware of how difficult it is to help students develop the skills to formulate their own inquiry. How can you both launch students into their own explorations and ensure academic rigor?

Doug: Our discussion of the ways of using the community inspired me to think about what we are actually trying to teach our students in our classrooms. I have loved believing that I teach my students to think independently and to formulate their own thoughts and hypotheses, but in reality I spend more time focusing on trivial material that will be on their next test.

Tracey: In our class last week, I was taken aback by the task of choosing our own project but then became very engaged in doing so. But that is a very different thing for students, especially students who are not used to choosing what they want to explore. I am not against having them decide; I just wonder about the tension between giving them direction and allowing freedom. How do we help them start without choosing for them?

Yet again, while we were unable to answer all of our questions, we seemed to have rediscovered the importance of asking. As with many other topics, we cannot discuss this one without seeing its connection to others. So many questions about implementation arise because each element of schooling affects all of the other elements. At this time, we began to feel the year's end approaching. As the reality of leaving this group and returning to our classrooms set in, these questions became more critical.

> *Chris:* Therein lies my frustration. I wanted to be in ETP because I felt like I was teaching in a vacuum. ETP has strengthened my desire to have teachers of like minds in my school. I do not feel that many of the topics we have discussed are best implemented in isolation in science class. The explorations and service learning session brought this idea home for me. I could very well continue my exploration of our local river and use this to teach science concepts. But the richness happens in the connections that are made with other disciplines and other teachers. Besides that, it's a lot of work for one teacher. So here I am; I want to do so many things. . . . How do we bring this experience back to our schools and how do we create a similar experience for teachers who do not have the opportunity to spend a year at Harvard?

Making the Circle Bigger: A Journey in the South Bronx

Susan McCray

Susan expanded on the writing she began in this seminar. During the spring semester she devoted an independent study with Eleanor to writing about a particularly painful and exhilarating year in her teaching. This became too big a piece to be included in this book. It has been published (McCray, 1996) in Journeys Through Our Classrooms, *and we greatly hope readers will look for it there. We print a short excerpt from it here.*

The following article describes some of my experiences while working as an Outward Bound instructor at the South Bronx High School in the school year 1991–92. For 4 years I co-taught a course that integrated the philosophy and methodology of experiential learning with a social studies and English curriculum. The course met daily for a double period, and the alumni of the class formed a club that gathered regularly after school. The school is located in Mott Haven, a section of the Bronx in New York City, and serves the local community, whose population is primarily Puerto Rican and Dominican, with a growing number of residents from other Latin American countries and a small percentage of African Americans. I myself, a white woman, grew up three subway stops and 15 minutes away on the Upper East Side of Manhattan. Ironically, the closer I became to these young people, the more profoundly aware I became of just how far those three subway stops and that 15 minutes are. So, while trying to capture the reality of our work together, I realize that even this description is from my own perspective.

Also, I am telling this story from journals and memory, and I know that recollection is inevitably a process of re-creation. In many instances, moments and individuals have wandered through my mind and landed on

---

This interlude is an excerpt from McCray, S. (1996). Making the circle bigger: A journey in the South Bronx. In D. Udall & A. Mednick (Eds.), *Journeys through our classrooms* (pp. 149–161). Dubuque, IA: Kendall-Hunt. Reprinted by permission of Kendall-Hunt.

the page in slightly new forms and sequences. The details may not be exact, but it is the essence of the story that remains most powerful. . . .

Each day I heard another story, because each young person has a story to tell. These stories were often of their personal struggles, but because of my students it seemed impossible for me to lose myself to despair. In response to the violence in their lives, the students of both the class and club decided to organize a series of events dedicated to peace and unity. They planned to build a park next to the school, Unity Park, and to prepare a week of workshops, assemblies, and speak-outs for the rest of the school. Their indefatigable spirit and our closeness as a community were the foundation of the park.

One morning I pushed through the school's heavy, metal front door and walked into Ramon's jubilant smile. He came gliding up and wrapped his arms around me. "Oh, Susan," he whispered in that gorgeous Dominican accent. He began to escort me to my office, "Susan, you look tired. You work too much. How are you? Did I tell you . . . ?" Ramon always had news that he dispatched with hushed intensity. His warmth was contagious. He led me up the stairs and right into "the desk mob." After 2 years of bureaucratic battles, I had procured a space for the program big enough to house an intimate miniclub. I said my hellos, letting the group of students know how sincerely good it was to see them. And before I could ask them where they were supposed to be, they assured me that Veronica had finished her test and Louis had been kicked out of science. After a long pause, Alex quickly added that he was on his way back to class. It was always tempting to let them stay; I sensed that they flocked here because they could find connection and caring. But I knew, and they knew, that they also had to hold each other accountable for all their academic responsibilities.

At this time of the year, in the middle of December, it was always hard to hold their attention in class. No matter how much I focused on creating a rich, dynamic curriculum, it always seemed to fall flat. The club attendance had dwindled, and the class was bored. I was bored and boring. We had completed our introductions, in which they interviewed each other and wrote biographies; we had been on our first backpacking trip; we had written a group contract; we had begun our cultural studies, and they had completed interviews of their own families. Now, in desperation (and lethargy), I tried having them write about themselves; I tried discussion; I even tried my old standby—debates. In reality, there was little solid content, nor was there an engaging project.

Fortunately, we put an urban exploration trip on the calendar. In many ways it became a pivotal juncture of the curriculum—an opportunity for them to see the lessons of the course as relevant and real. I hoped that studying other communities would help us develop ideas for our project. We would go to another neighborhood in the city, the Lower East Side of Manhattan, searching for examples of parks and murals and meeting people who could be role models and inspire our work.

But it took a lot of convincing. Students wondered why we should bother wandering the streets of Manhattan, a place they knew and sometimes feared. On a school trip they assumed there was always the chance of danger or, worse, ridicule from strangers. The Lower East Side is demographically and physically similar to the South Bronx, but once we were there it was far enough away from home that we could enter with an explorer's perspective, both anxious and open.

I helped them find their way to a collection of murals known on the Lower East Side as the "protest murals," but when we arrived and found the gate locked, we just stood on the corner aimlessly. We had spent hours in class practicing approaching and interviewing people in the street, but still the students were hesitant and resistant about moving beyond our group. Garfield took the initiative. He walked toward a man sitting on a nearby stoop, while the rest of the group stood riveted, watching and waiting in awe. This is not something a young Black Jamaican man wearing baggy jeans and a baseball cap does outside of his own neighborhood in New York City. The time passed; Garfield continued talking with this man, while the rest of us stared at Garfield. Eventually he took his journal out and began writing. Then he and the man began walking back toward us. "This is David." Garfield introduced each of us, and then he told us that David knew all about the neighborhood. He had been homeless for years, but he had spent that time in the area and even had a key to the park. He had helped build it, had organized a rally when the city officials threatened to destroy it, and was continuing to watch over it. So we followed David into his garden and spent the next hour of this bitter cold December day standing beneath the huge murals hearing about his life and his views of the homeless situation and of the social and political history of the community.

Later Hugo, who had recently come to this country from El Salvador, captured the moment in writing. He was usually so quiet and shy. He rarely spoke or wrote in class; but now he responded to a phrase in the mural painted beneath a crystal ball: "La Lucha Continua means that the struggle never ends. You always have to keep fighting for a better future. Never give up on life. Always keep trying to be the best." This is why I leave the classroom with my students; I could never have planned this experience.

As we walked away and left David sitting on his bench, Garfield pulled on the "hoody" of his full-length Fat Goose jacket and wrapped his arm around Carmen's shoulders. For that hour none of us had noticed the cold.

What Happened to Vivaldi?

Duane Grobman II and Suzy Ort

April 21

"I heard your question in that meeting. I worked at a Coalition school, too, in New Mexico."

"Really? That's great. We'll have to get together to talk."

"Yeah, I'd love to talk to someone who was at another Coalition school in another part of the country."

"Me too. How 'bout next week . . . ?"

From the beginning Duane and Suzy had a "coalition."

As new students, we met during an orientation week meeting. A question Suzy raised in the meeting revealed the connection that inspired the conversation cited above: "Do people here talk much about the Coalition of Essential Schools [CES]?"

This organization was formed in 1984 at Brown University by Theodore Sizer as a school–university partnership committed to improving the quality of education in schools throughout the United States. It began as an attempt to put into practice the ideas explored in Sizer's (1984) book, *Horace's Compromise*, and a set of "common principles" (see Figure 10). The Coalition grew largely out of the project, A Study of High Schools (1984), an extensive, 5-year inquiry into U.S. secondary education conducted from 1979 to 1984. The study identified five "imperatives" for improving schools in this country:

- Give room to teachers and students to work and learn in their own appropriate ways.
- Insist that students clearly exhibit mastery of their school work.
- Get the incentives right for students and teachers.
- Focus the students' work on the use of their minds.
- Keep the structure simple and flexible.

As teachers in Coalition schools, we were asked to lead a session on school reform and specifically our experience with the CES. Over the first 6 months of ETP many of our classmates had engaged us in one-on-one conversations about the Coalition, and we looked forward to sharing our stories as well as discussing our lingering questions with the group.

We approached this task with genuine excitement and an awareness of the challenges inherent in sharing our experiences and, at the same time, articulating the principles that inform the Coalition as a whole. First and foremost, we hoped to engage our classmates in a critical dialogue about issues of school reform. Stemming from that discussion, we wanted to offer two examples of school reform efforts—namely, the Coalition and the Kansas City (Missouri) initiative. The former advocates that the process of school reform take place school by school, as a cooperative decision and effort of parents, teachers, administrators, and students. The latter emerged from a Missouri court decision addressing school desegregation and school financing throughout the state. As a result of this decision, approximately $1.2 billion were invested in a districtwide school improvement plan.

In planning, we faced the perennial teacher dilemma of what to cover and how to do it creatively in a limited amount of time. "Less is more," says Sizer. In our session, we wanted to simulate a model of a Coalition classroom. We wanted to include the possibility for "multiple entry points" into material that would be relevant and interesting, the cultivation of student engagement and active participation, the notion that we were "coaches" or facilitators of learning rather than omniscient transmitters of information, and finally, the variety of "activities" found in many Coalition classrooms. We wanted to create a comfortable atmosphere where people felt excited and ready to engage in serious dialogue about serious issues.

We brainstormed creative ways to begin our session. In talking about the prospect of using classical music, we discovered that we had both taught a lesson involving Vivaldi's *The Four Seasons*. We were amazed how elementary and high school students alike had enjoyed Vivaldi and marveled at his use of sounds to portray seasons. As the snow outside our ETP classroom continued to fall and accumulate (in April!), we thought his "Winter" piece would be an appropriate and innovative way to launch our discussion. Following this, our plans to stimulate discussion included a short videoclip about the Kansas City school reform initiative, a quick brainstorm of "what do you wonder about the Coalition?", ample time for deep discussion and a group reading of "Winter Oak" (Nagibin, 1987), a wonderful story of a teacher's own "reform." All of this would culminate in processing and reflection at the end. What we didn't want to do was a 2-hour lecture on the Coalition or a reenactment of *Horace's Compromise*.

FIGURE 10. The Common Principles, Coalition of Essential Schools

1. The school should focus on **helping adolescents learn to use their minds well.** Schools should not attempt to be "comprehensive" if such a claim is made at the expense of the school's central intellectual purpose.

2. The school's goals should be simple: that each student **master a limited number of essential skills and areas of knowledge.** While these skills and areas will, to varying degrees, reflect the traditional academic disciplines, the program's design should be shaped by the intellectual and imaginative powers and competencies that students need, rather than necessarily by "subjects" as conventionally defined. The aphorism "less is more" should dominate: Curricular decisions should be guided by the aim of thorough student mastery and achievement rather than by an effort merely to cover content.

3. The school's **goals should apply** to all students, while the means of these goals will vary as those students themselves vary. School practice should be tailor-made to meet the needs of every group or class of adolescents.

4. **Teaching and learning should be personalized** to the maximum feasible extent. Efforts should be directed toward a goal that no teacher have direct responsibility for more than 80 students. To capitalize on this personalization, decisions about the details of the course of study, the use of students' and teachers' time, and the choice of teaching materials and specific pedagogies must be unreservedly placed in the hands of the principal and staff.

5. **The governing practical metaphor of the school should be student-as-worker** rather than the more familiar metaphor of teacher-as-deliverer-of-instructional-services. Accordingly, a prominent pedagogy will be coaching, to provoke students to learn how to learn and thus to teach themselves.

6. Students entering secondary school studies are those who can show competence in language and elementary mathematics. Students of traditional high school age but not yet at appropriate levels of competence to enter secondary school studies will be provided intensive remedial work to assist them quickly to meet those standards. **The diploma should be awarded upon a successful final demonstration of mastery** for graduation—an "exhibition." This exhibition by the student of his or her grasp of the central skills and knowledge of the school's program may be jointly administered by the faculty and by higher authorities. As the diploma is awarded when earned, the school's program proceeds with no strict age grading and with no system of "credits earned" by "time spent" in class. The emphasis is on the students' demonstration that they can do important things.

7. **The tone of the school** should explicitly and self-consciously stress values of **unanxious expectation** ("I won't threaten you but I expect much of you"), of **trust** (until abused), and of **decency** (the values of fairness, generosity, and tolerance). Incentives appropriate to the school's particular students and teachers should be emphasized, and parents should be treated as essential collaborators.

8. **The principal and teachers should perceive themselves as generalists first** (teachers and scholars in general education) and specialists second (experts in but one particular discipline). Staff should expect multiple obligations (teacher–counselor–manager) and a sense of commitment to the entire school.

9. Ultimate administrative and budget targets should include, in addition to **total student loads per teacher of 80 or fewer pupils, substantial time for collective planning by teachers, competitive salaries for staff, and an ultimate per-pupil cost** not to exceed that at traditional schools by more than 10 percent. To accomplish this, administrative plans may have to show the phased reduction or elimination of some services now provided students in many traditional comprehensive secondary schools.

Any list of such brevity and specificity begs for elaboration, and it is this elaboration that must first engage the energies of each Essential school. The process of designing programs and putting them into place will take several years, and the inevitable adjustments then required will consume some years after that. Due to its complexity, school redesign is a slow and often costly business. And due to the need to adapt each design to its own constituency of students, teachers, parents, and neighborhoods and to create a strong sense of ownership of it by those who are involved, this redesign must be largely done at the level of the individual school—even as that school adheres to the principles and standards common among the Coalition member schools.

In reflecting on our facilitation of this class, we realized that the dilemmas we faced mirrored those faced by many teachers. We had great plans. We wanted to do it all. Yet time became our foe! We didn't get to half of what we planned, and our "less" became much, much "more." In the end we never even got to discuss why Vivaldi had started us off.

In the midst of laying those "best-laid plans," how do you choose the most "essential" questions, the most salient information to address? How is the information/material that you choose best shared? Does being student-centered preclude any spotlight on the teacher's own knowledge and experi-

ence? When is "less" too little and when is "more" too much? Where is the
balance between breadth and depth?

These questions about teaching and learning lie at the heart of school
reform as espoused by the Coalition. They echo the teacher voices we often
heard in our schools. To us, they also reinforce the crucial role that teachers
must play in systemic school reform efforts.

Many of these questions had been on the minds of our ETP classmates
prior to our session.

> *Chris:* I have this ideal vision of everything coming together and every
> teacher sharing a common vision. I look forward to hearing and partic-
> ipating in the session that Duane and Suzy have prepared for us. I am
> at the point where I need to know a little more about how school re-
> form comes about. What does it look and feel like, and what does the
> product taste like? I know that this next session will probably continue
> to build my desire to do more things at my school.

Some thought about how this "ideal vision" might be achieved.

> *Doug:* It really seems like the easiest thing would be to start from
> scratch with a brand-new school and a devoted and interested faculty.
> Of course, financial restrictions would not permit this, but if I ever
> win the lottery maybe that's what I will do (of course, my first step
> would be to hire all my fellow ETPers).

> *Chris:* If a school were to seriously think about reform, I think they
> need to think about what good things (curriculum, extracurricular ac-
> tivities) must stay and what good things must go. This seems to be the
> only way to pare down the demands placed on teachers.

It could be argued that the approach taken by the Kansas City Schools,
as portrayed in the video segment, was a combination of Chris's and Doug's
approaches. That is, add to the good things found in the school, eliminate
the bad things, and relish the benefits of a lottery-sized influx of money.
This straightforward approach elicited strong reactions from other members of our class:

> *Eleanor:* The videoclip was pretty amazing. . . . I appreciated the is-
> sues that it raised. The sorts of things that money can, and in this case
> did, buy (musical instruments, pleasant space) and the sorts of things
> that it may or may not be able to buy, but in any event in this case
> didn't (thoughtfulness about teaching). I was annoyed at the single-

dimensioned thinking (in this journalistic account) about how to tell whether changes are making any difference (test scores) and the overlooking of the statistics telling of fewer dropouts and less vandalism.

Tracey: I also really liked seeing the [video]clip — I had heard of it and was eager to see it for myself. It worries me that such journalism appears on TV — I know that I heard from a few people (nonteachers) who had seen it, and their reactions were along the lines of "See! More money is not the answer!" They did not seem to recognize the incompleteness of the piece. . . . It's no wonder that we have no books or paper in our schools.

The lack of teacher involvement in the Kansas City reform initiative drew strong reactions from ETPers. On the other hand, we recognized the time demands placed on teachers involved in school reform.

Time and the teacher are partners in the experience of learning and teaching. Often their relationship can be described as rocky. Time can be the teacher's best friend (what greater reward than to see a student blossom over several years?), but, more frequently, it is a stubborn and daunting foe. Reflections from our classmates spoke of this noteworthy partner and the effects its presence had both on our evening's session and on the dynamic between time and the teacher in a Coalition school.

Eleanor: I can't believe how fast 3 hours go. Suzy and Duane barely got to begin — but there was a whole lot more planned . . . (I think), and suddenly it was over. I know that one of the things planned was the reading of the story ["Winter Oak"] together. And that another was some attention to the music that was playing.

Chris: I was most impressed with the amount of time required of a teacher working in a Coalition school. I am reminded of the problem facing the team of teachers with whom I work. . . . We have no time to plan, and we have no time to "get through" the curriculum that our district expects us to cover. I know and believe that "getting through" and "covering" are not politically correct ideas, but they are realistic aspects of the mindset of teachers within schools.

Jane: I sit in meeting after meeting, discussing this survey and that committee and leaving with a question mark about how my time in these meetings helps my students. In a Coalition school the purpose seems clearer.

We would agree, as teachers who have spent some years in Coalition schools, that the purposes behind a teacher's use of time are often clearer there. However, as our classmates pointed out, and as we can further attest, the perpetual problems inherent in the relationship between teacher and time have not been resolved completely.

Chris: It doesn't seem as if the Coalition schools described by our presenters have solved the problem of time. Taking risks is a wonderful maxim, but having the time to take a well-thought-out, calculated risk results in a more successful project than does jumping blindly into risky activity. As I talk with teachers in Brookline about Coalition schools and my desire to have our school follow the lead or actually become a Coalition school, I run into this issue of time over and over again.

Many of the demands placed on the teacher do not remain within the walls of the school building at the end of the day. Often they follow the teacher home. Some of these demands are to be expected and accepted by anyone filling the shoes of the one called teacher. Yet how much is realistic to expect? How much is fair for a teacher to accept? This is a question that members of our group wrestled with throughout the year and that became most amplified in our session on school reform.

Doug: I would be hard-pressed to spend more time and energy and thought on my students without sacrificing my family life and necessary relaxation time. I feel that I have a healthy outlook on life and that I am at peace with who I am, but I know that I would lose my spiritual comfort if I were to change my priorities dramatically. I don't feel that it is worth it for myself, nor do I think that it is the right message to send to my students.

Duane: I particularly appreciated Doug's comments—honest reflections about the concern and reality of teacher burnout. I think that the demands of a Coalition school can position one for that. I also think a traditional school addicted to the status quo and fearful of change can position a teacher for burnout as well.

Susan: I so want to be doing the work that I am passionately committed to, inspired by, and fulfilled by. I know that I am happiest when I feel as though I am making a difference. But I also want to have a balance in my life. I know that I have a tendency to immerse myself completely in my work. For the last 4 years, the South Bronx High

School/Outward Bound Center was my air and water, heart and soul. And I would not trade away any piece of that experience. But, now, I would like to be able to maintain that fulfilling intensity while also nourishing my relationships, building a personal community, and pursuing other vital interests. And I want to believe that all this is possible.

When it comes to time and the teacher, we all want to believe it is possible to balance professional dedication with an intact personal life. The question of "how" continues to pose the most formidable challenge.

As mentioned earlier, in planning our session we also faced the challenge of deciding what material to select and how to present it. As the topic of our class was school reform or, essentially, "doing things differently," it is ironic that our presentation was probably one of the most "traditional" classes that we had in ETP. Since conversations around school reform often focus on the importance of being "student-centered" and using constructivist instructional practices, we were feeling somewhat uneasy about the format of our session:

Suzy: The planning of the class brought up many teaching dilemmas. What to focus on? Where is the balance between shifting gears and leaving the time to really explore a topic? How best to "deliver" "new" information? How to make it as discovery-oriented as possible? I had the realization that discovery-oriented stuff happens only over time. How easily that is sacrificed in the interest of conveying information. How soon we (I) forget.

Several of our classmates' reactions, however, helped us understand that sometimes a teacher-centered class can be effective.

Jorge: The format of asking Suzy and Duane questions was the appropriate one. Listening to their personal experiences gave me a good idea of what "reform" schools are all about.

Eleanor: I loved hearing Suzy and Duane talk about their teaching. (More, I think, than hearing them talk about their schools.)

Tracey: The session was clearly different from previous ones in that it was very "teacher-centered." However, I think that was not only OK, but appropriate. While it would have been interesting to talk about our ideas for school reform (and I would still like to), the opportunity to take advantage of their [Suzy and Duane's] firsthand knowledge was well worth the time. . . .

In my years at Clara Barton [High School], we heard "student-centered, cooperative learning, active, no lecture . . . " over and over again. While I agree with the importance of student-centered, active learning, I still feel that there remains a purpose for an occasional lecture-style class, or if not a lecture, then one in which the teacher provides most of the information and responds to student questions. Sometimes, in the midst of all the "new ideas" about teaching, I feel hesitant to say that! Sometimes, I would begin a lesson and students would ask questions, and the period would be taken over by such a teacher-dominated question-and-answer-type class. If my assistant principal had walked in, he would have been extremely upset, and I don't understand why.

Tracey's comments in particular speak to the heart of school reform, at least in the way that we interpret Sizer's ideas as embodied in the Coalition of Essential Schools. Sizer does not present a "model" for an "Essential" school or a blueprint for "Sizerian" pedagogy—do it this way—active, cooperative, interdisciplinary—always or else. His pedagogical strategies are secondary to the notion of teachers questioning their practice deeply and wondering, in the same ways they would want their students to do, about the best way to structure a particular lesson. This idea of "reflective practice"—self-assessment, collaboration/reassessment, risk taking, and vision—can be thought of as the four seasons of a teacher's yearly growth. Perhaps we know better now why Vivaldi got us started and more clearly what direction to go in the efforts to reform our schools.

A Game of Cards

JANE KAYS

May 6

This was the last session of the year. A week later we would gather at Eleanor's house for our final celebration. Since September we had spent many hours together. We had met for 3 hours every other week; we'd met on two separate occasions during our "off" weeks to continue conversations related to class topics; we spent an evening playing volleyball followed by dinner and talk at a local restaurant; and we'd had a holiday party at Tracey's house in January. It seemed as though the fourteen of us, although so different in our professional backgrounds, were now united by attempts to understand and appreciate those differences. Through our written reflections, class sessions, and informal gatherings, we had come to know each other. Perhaps we were ready to approach a potentially difficult topic.

Our final class was designed to allow all of us to think about ourselves and our own attitudes about multiculturalism. Elissa and I decided that we would not focus on how to use a multicultural approach but rather promote a discussion about its importance. We felt this was an important step to take before designing lessons or activities.

The two of us were philosophically bound by our personal commitment for the need to understand multiculturalism from a broad perspective rather than some of the more restrictive interpretations of the concept. Multiculturalism should and could mean more than celebrating famous birthdays or focusing on thinking about our differences only during certain months. Instead, we wanted our classmates to think about and discuss how we can create an inclusive atmosphere for all of our students; we wondered if we really "see" who sits before us in our classrooms.

Elissa and I began meeting to plan the class. First, we chose readings by scholars who have worked toward creating a multicultural environment in schools. Articles by Maxine Greene (1993), Lisa Delpit (1988), and James Banks (1977) were the only homework assignment. We then planned a brief card game activity and a short in-class reading as entry points into our discussion.

After three planning meetings, we met with Eleanor to set forth our plan. Eleanor was interested in our approach and in one idea in particular.

I had remembered a reflection written by Rosario on March 23 in which she explored the reasons she does not participate often in our class discussions. She probed the possibility that being Colombian might be a factor. She wrote about feeling left out and different. This seemed like a very vivid way for us to address the topic. We decided to use that portion of Rosario's reflection with the group. Eleanor not only supported this but also told us she was disappointed in herself for not having already done something about Rosario's journal entry:

> I wondered why I didn't participate that much. I keep feeling kind of awkward. It is difficult for me to express myself both in ideas and in emotions. But I really don't know why. Perhaps it's something with culture, with not identifying completely with what is being described. And yet, I love to learn from listening . . . I guess I just feel I have nothing to add, no experience that can be thought-provoking or exciting to think about. I really don't know!

Next we told Rosario about our idea and asked her permission to use her entry anonymously. She said we could. Then, with Eleanor, we discussed how to present the question that would accompany Rosario's reflection. We decided we would ask the group what they would do if one of their students wrote the passage and lead into a discussion about the need for teachers to be aware of who their students are.

Our introduction to the discussion was a card game. The game is played in groups of four. All the players know that the object of the game is to win as many tricks as possible; but each table has received a different set of written rules to be memorized at the onset and talking is not permitted. After four quick hands, one person from each group moves to the next table, and the playing resumes. Thus, each table becomes a place where plays become confusing when, for example, one of the players thinks that aces are high and the other three players think that aces are low.

We wanted the game to be a way for us to think about how it might feel to be in a group where we do not fully understand how the group works. Metaphorically, this could be anywhere from the classroom to a citizens' group. However, different members of the group expressed a variety of views about this activity. For some the metaphor worked, and they described feelings of exclusion and aggression, a loss of confidence and identity, not caring and giving up. For a few it was simply a game of cards, and fun was the outcome. As leaders of the session, we felt some tension in the air with these two vastly different responses. Some people saw the game as we had; others did not care to address multiculturalism through the card-game metaphor. We had looked forward to having a wonderful discussion about multiculturalism, but this early signal led us to believe that this was not a topic with which everyone felt comfortable.

Perhaps that was a moment when *we* needed to look more closely at who sat before us that evening — ironically, the very message we hoped to discuss about our respective students. However, though we listened to what our classmates offered, we moved on. Rosario's journal entry was meant to return our thoughts to our classrooms and our obligations as teachers who find ourselves in the midst of diverse student populations. We gave everyone a copy and asked what they would do as teachers if one of their students had written it.

Members of the group responded immediately. There were concerns about timing. If this were at the beginning of the year, a group activity about everyone's culture might be appropriate. However, students might not have enough trust in their classmates and the teacher at the beginning of the year, and it might be wise to wait. At this point we told the group that it was written in the middle of the year. There were new replies based on this bit of information. Now one classmate felt that this required speaking individually to the student; others pointed out that any approach would depend upon the particular student. The group's reactions were sincere. To have a student feel this way was a serious matter. They tapped many possibilities in their attempt to find a way to include a student who, at times, felt excluded. Perhaps culture was not the issue for this student. Maybe it was a psychological issue. The conversation was so animated, a mixture of dovetailed agreements combined with contrary opinions, that neither Elissa nor I noticed that some members of the group were not participating. At the same time, Eleanor intervened to try to take the emphasis away from what might be seen as a problem student and make sure that we addressed the teacher's responsibility. She asked, "Would this entry cause a teacher to think more about how she runs her class and how she makes her students feel? Should she bring the incident to the class, try to design classes better, or act differently?"

Prior to Eleanor's questions, Rosario found herself in an awkward position. It felt as if the discussion carried sensitive implications. Although we had briefly discussed our plans with her, there was no way for any of us to know how it would feel to be talked about while being present and remain anonymous at the same time. Removing her name certainly did not protect her. And she did not even feel free to tell the group she was the writer. I cannot explain exactly what made this situation difficult for Rosario. However, something struck a sensitive chord, and her eyes filled with tears.

That evening the class sat in a large square formation, and Rosario sat opposite Elissa and me. On an adjacent side sat Eleanor. Amid the flurry of responses, silence suddenly permeated the area where Elissa and I were sitting. For a moment we heard nothing. We seemed locked into place, wanting to reach out to Rosario, needing to confer with Eleanor, but temporarily feeling restrained and caught in the unexpected emotion of the moment. Elissa and I deliberated, and in an instant we passed a note to Eleanor saying that we must reveal the author of the entry. Eleanor sent a note to Rosario, clearing the way for telling the class that the journal entry was Rosario's.

At that point, a stronger discussion evolved. Some accused us of deception while others supported the activity. Mark missed this session. He listened to it on tape and wrote the following:

> *Mark:* It seemed to me that the issue that most concerned people was how Jane and Elissa used Rosario's own experiences and narrative reflections in their discussion. As Rosario became emotional over what had been, at times, a difficult year (from the perspective of someone from another culture at the Ed. school), there was concern in the group that Rosario's piece had been used improperly. It seems to me that what was at issue here was how best to honor and respect a person's private thoughts, while still including them in our learning. The issue is at base whether personal things can be kept separate from "curriculum" when it comes to multicultural questions or, at least, how separate we must keep them.

Mark speaks of separating the personal from the curriculum when it comes to multicultural questions. Many layers of the personal became tangled during our session. Elissa, Eleanor, and I thought that Rosario's entry would be helpful because it represented a situation in which all of us had actually been participants. We wanted a discussion about the multicultural situation we ourselves were experiencing. However, once Rosario was identified as the author, we learned that we had unintentionally added another layer to that experience. We had created two groups—one group who knew and one group who didn't know whose entry it was. We had been playing out our own game of cards. The group who knew had recognized the reflection as one written by Rosario and hardly participated in the discussion. Their responses were stifled. If they admitted they knew who wrote the entry, they might interfere with the activity. Should they pretend to not know and respond accordingly? Others, who did not know who wrote it, endeavored to determine what to do about this anonymous student. They fervently tried to understand and address the incident. What we had were two groups participating in the same activity under different guidelines.

For the second time that evening emotions ran high. For some it was as powerful and thought-provoking as it had been for Eleanor. They came to realize that they had not acted in March as tonight they said a teacher ought to act. Others felt set up. People admitted feeling awkward, uncomfortable, and weird. And for Elissa and me it felt as though we were being attacked. Both groups voiced some measure of discontent. Elissa and I never meant to stir the emotions that fueled that session. Our intention was to ignite thoughts about multicultural education. However, this topic can be explosive. Still, one may argue that it was not the topic, but the manner in which it was presented. In any event, we can use this experience as another piece in the quest for understanding ourselves and the students who sit before us.

> *Tracey:* I left our session on multiculturalism with a lot of mixed feelings. I felt badly that so many people were upset when we left. I'm not bothered by the fact that people were emotional but by the fact that so much was left unresolved. The session was wonderfully planned — the beginning activity was fun and contained great comparisons to the issue of multiculturalism. The discussion based on Rosario's comments was valuable because it personalized the issue and gave it a lot of meaning. Unfortunately, not everyone had the kind of reaction I did. I felt uncomfortable because I, too, had read that piece before, and I did not pick up on what it really said. I am more convinced than ever that it *is* vital to be aware of these issues in the classroom. Unfortunately, I still remain uncertain as to how to actually address them.

The class ended with our circle-of-comments routine. Most everyone was supportive of our efforts, although some people passed, which was not uncommon during this practice. Then people lingered and left more slowly than usual. Burry stayed for a long time to compose the following letter. He wanted to be sure it would be in our student mailboxes the following morning.

May 6   10:35 PM

Dear Jane and Elissa,

Many times in my life I have been confronted with the uncomfortable. Very often how I am confronted with it determines whether I will simply be able to pass it off as an intellectual exercise or whether I will have to deal with it and possibly learn in a real way. Tonight's class for me was an experience in the latter.

So often I am reminded that all real growth is painful. The two of you did a truly courageous thing. You could easily have couched to-night in easy-to-swallow aphorisms, and we all would have nodded our heads, agreed that multicultural education is a good thing, and gone on our ways, unchanged.

But your lesson required me, at least, to come to grips with this is-sue on a far more personal level. I am sure that I will not resolve how I feel about multiculturalism education or its philosophy in a few short hours or a few short years. I cannot, however, walk away from it.

This cannot be a "safe" topic, glibly dealt with and easily dis-missed. In your choice of pedagogy, you honored us by being willing to risk incurring the great emotions surrounding this topic and being willing to risk our relationships, so that we might face it head on and grow as a result. This is too important a topic for us to stay safe and unaffected. It is the greatest measure of your caring for us that you put friendship on the line to teach us. For me, nothing could better de-fine a master teacher. Thank you for that. It was powerful; it was hard; and it caused me to think.

Regards,

Burry

Outsiders Still

JANE KAYS

This interlude is yet another example of how it feels to belong to the outside group.

For many years I taught in neighborhoods that one would describe as ghettos or, in today's P.C. terminology, the inner city, a somewhat kinder way to talk about that aspect of our society that stands apart from the "outer city"—dilapidated homes, projects that seem uninhabitable, and streets littered with clues of poverty. The inner city was home to my students, perhaps not what middle-class standards equate with comfort, but here was the place that belonged to them. Nonetheless, there seems to be a universal feeling about the place we call "home." There are feelings of comfort and security that negate any designs that wealth may inscribe upon the walls that wrap themselves around us.

In the days before desegregation, when neighborhoods and schools were synonymous, my students and I often ventured outside into their neighborhood—sometimes to the local library, or to the nearest bus stop on the way to a museum. The school where I taught was surrounded by the children's residences but also bordered a shopping area. A busy intersection separated us from the merchants, as well as the bus stop and the iron skeleton stairs that clinked upwards to the trains that traversed the city—inner and outer. On our excursions we'd pass people who were on their way to do whatever the morning calls them to do. Crossing the street with 30 third graders was easy. Cars would stop and arms would beckon us to pass in front of their vehicles, allowing the endless trail of little feet to safely negotiate sidewalk to sidewalk. We often interacted with the neighbors.

"Well, well, where y'all goin' this morning?"

"Good morning, good morning," we'd chant and wave.

There was never a time when men and women, young and old, who lived around the school hesitated to exchange a greeting with the children and myself. I never regarded their greetings to me, an outsider by my skin color, as extraordinary. I did not seek to explain the ordinary friendliness of the neighbors through any social, political, or economic analysis. Their greetings were basic gestures, welcomed by my black students and myself, their white teacher.

After the courts ended school segregation, my school continued to service many neighborhood children, perhaps 50 to 60%. The rest of the children who attended lived in different parts of the city. My class became a mixture of hues and whos. Outwardly, their skin color revealed some of their background. Inwardly, their language, their families, and their customs colored who they were. For the first time, I was teaching children whose first language was not English. Lizette from Peru spoke English the way I spoke Spanish, with a struggle. I often wondered what the smile in her ebony eyes was saying about my Spanish. We were both challenged in our attempts to find a common ground between our inner and outer speech. One or two of the students were of Irish descent, and most were African Americans. With this somewhat diverse group of children, I continued the same excursions through the neighborhood and encountered the same friendly greetings from the local residents. Our diversity did not interrupt the cordiality we received.

Now, many years later, I still teach in the city, but in a different school in a less shabby neighborhood. By contrast, it is pristine—neat yards, neat single-family homes on tidy streets. However, this is not a neighborhood school, as fewer than 10% of the students live nearby. Most of my students live in less privileged settings and arrive at school on a bus. If there is a feeling of hominess, it is only within the school, in the classroom, or within a particular circle of friends. Without a shopping area nearby, the area seems sedate, with only the children's voices charging off the school buses to infuse the neighborhood with vitality.

I still rely on neighborhood outings and public transportation as a way to enrich the curriculum. One advantage to teaching in a city is the proximity of many cultural institutions. There are museums, the theater, and the ballet, just to name a few, and very little that is not accessible by bus or train. I also use the public library as a resource, hoping it may influence my students to consider reading as a pastime. For those who are not easily influenced, the library offers exhibits, free movies, story hours, and a safe place to spend an afternoon. Ever since I was young, libraries to me have been like candy stores with so much that looks so tempting. I used to imagine reading all the juvenile fiction, beginning with the *A*'s and plowing through to *Z*. My goal for my students is that they will, at the very least, seek out their local libraries as a resource and a place of comfort.

When I began planning where I would take this year's class, I faced a dilemma. How could we walk to this neighborhood's library, when the neighborhood belonged to only two or three of the students? If one of my goals is to familiarize the children with their local library, was it sensible to visit a place that would be inaccessible to a 9-year-old who lived on the other side of the city? I decided to plan one trip to the closest library before I considered other visits. New to the area, I asked the principal where that library was. Before she revealed the location, she momentarily shared her feeling that the children did not seem welcome there. Without reaching for the gory and apparent details, I immediately formulated the year's trips. Of course we would visit that library and show how "welcome" we could be. But beyond the business of diplomacy, we would visit every child's neighborhood and their own local library.

The address list of the students revealed that they lived in six different zones that were serviced by six different branches of the public library. Using a public transportation schedule, I tallied the fares for the four trips (two libraries were within walking distance). I then wrote and received a $150 minigrant to fund the transportation cost. The school librarian called each library to arrange times throughout the year for our visits, about one visit every 6 weeks.

Our first excursion would take us on a nostalgic visit to the neighborhood where I began my teaching career. A drop of fear punctuated my memory as violent images from the news blurred the cordial relationships I remembered. However, excitement prevailed, and we all eagerly anticipated the trip. Many children were eager to show me where they lived, and I would show them "my old school."

Before our first venture, we discussed bus etiquette and sidewalk etiquette — offer your seat to the elderly and to people with young children; do not pull at the bushes and do not walk in anyone's yard; and stop at each crossing. As we snaked our way to the bus stop, three blocks away, the air was crisp. Leaves crunched under our feet, and the sun filtered through the remaining foliage. Beams of light met the many freckles that covered Sean, whose family had come here from Ireland 2 years ago. Shadows danced behind Gabriel and Tyrone, who led the line. Their families were from Jamaica and Haiti, and the boys often reminisced about their sunshine island homes. Natalia captured the attention of the back of the line with her story about her recent trip to Mississippi to a family reunion. Dania and Yessenia alternated between Spanish and English in their talk about the neighborhood. The 23 of us seemed to mesh with the day as our voices blended with the crisp air, crunching footsteps, and streams of sunlight.

How naive I was the first time out in this neighborhood, where residents take such pride in their property, where flower beds lie clear of brown leaves and shrubs are shaped, where homes are freshly painted and dogs are fenced in their yards, where sidewalks are swept and neatly curtained windows accentuate the flavor of the area.

As the children waited at the first crosswalk, I inched off the curb, instinctively knowing that the approaching sedan would pause and wave us ahead. Instead, the driver glared and smeared his tires around the corner in front of us. I'm sure the children noticed nothing but the freedom of the autumn air; I felt the sting of a time two decades ago when whites were forced to send their children to schools in black neighborhoods and accept outsiders into their neighborhood schools. Rather than send their children to a location they did not prefer, many fled the system and saturated the local parochial schools. However, they could not deny black students the right to attend the schools that they abandoned.

Now, 25 years later, the attitudes that purged the schools of their whiteness are as strong as they were when busing was first implemented. I knew the driver who denied our passing was not harried by time but irked by the outsiders who continue to invade his space.

Finis Origine Pendet

Duane Grobman II and Christopher Whitbeck

May 12

Our final gathering was a potluck dinner in Eleanor's home. This was a time to celebrate our year, to reflect, to share "what's next" for each of us, and to say farewell. We clanked our glasses in a toast to a school year well spent together, 9 months of learning and laughing, inquiring and investigating, expressing and exploring our ongoing questions about teaching.

While the food and conversation had been plentiful, we were each, in our own way, conscious of the emotional and pedagogical debate that had colored our class session just one week earlier. As we settled into Eleanor's living room, that consciousness took center stage for some. We were aware that yes, we were here to celebrate and to say good-bye, but we were also aware that significant loose ends lingered.

Our plan for the evening called for each person to share their plans for the upcoming year, within a 3-minute time limit. Our original tales of how we got into teaching had taken two nights, and this 3-minute time limit was an attempt to hear from everyone in 1 hour. A tape recorder ran, as it did in many of our sessions, capturing these stories for further reflection. Since this was our last gathering and no journals would follow, the quotations are transcripts from the evening's discussion.

Jorge began by sharing his thoughts about our previous class session. In that session Jorge had been relatively quiet. During the 7 days that followed, Jorge had reflected on our class's experience discussing multiculturalism.

> *Jorge:* Rosario and I talked yesterday about what we were going to say today. We're worried about leaving an impression that we're upset or made to feel uncomfortable. We don't want that because as you said there were a lot of questions for the class to investigate. We couldn't have learned it without the people that are here. I think the most important word is *respect*. It's hard to understand. . . . Each one of you

helped Rosario and me learn things. There are several different examples. I can say that Burry invited me and my wife for Christmas, that's wonderful. "Oh, come for an American Christmas." Each one of you have had something special for a different time of the year that you shared with us. So we want to say that we are very, very happy with the group and we are very grateful.

It hadn't been the entire group's intention to continue the discussion about our feelings from the multicultural class, but Jorge's comments raised the concern about weaving together loose ends and led to the question, "Is anyone still uncomfortable or upset about what happened last week?" There were still things to learn from one another. Eleanor and Rosario were the first to respond.

Eleanor: It almost seems not totally necessary at the moment, because we all seem to be in such good cheer, but I still want to say a few things. One is that whatever feelings seemed to be directed at Jane and Elissa last time should have been directed at me, too. We were the three who planned this session, and I feel that I was exonerated from whatever anger people were feeling. I also wanted to say that in the planning, we didn't set out to make people feel that we were putting one over on them. It's because of the trust in this group that we undertook to do what we did. We took Rosario's statement, and we were sort of fooling people. I don't know what word to use, but I'll use *fooling* to stand for whatever it was. We thought that if we had a general discussion about multiculturalism, it would be very easy for us all to say the right things. But we thought that we might show that it's easy to say the right things and yet not necessarily act the way that we believe. [The way we tried to show that] might have been a mistake.

One thing that we didn't think of was how many people would recognize the selection as Rosario's, and so half of the group was in and half of the group was out. That was too bad.

We never intended to have people say something that they wish they hadn't. We did it so that each of us could look honestly at how we respond to the multiculturalism within our own group. I had read Rosario's journal and had not responded, and that seemed to me to be a very powerful way to bring home the issue. It's certainly true that since it was powerful to me, knowing that it was Rosario's, it would have been possible to do it quite openly with the whole group. We could have said, "Here's Rosario, who wrote this, and what did we do about it?" We weren't trying to have people "caught out" saying things that would make them feel uncomfortable with each other. We thought that it might make people feel uncomfortable with *themselves* and that that might be productive. So, I'm sorry for whatever misjudgment there was, but it was done because there was this group in which we had so much confidence that we thought we would try it. We didn't mean to betray the trust; we thought it was building on the trust.

Rosario: I felt that the decision had a lot to do with respect for me. You cared very much whether I would feel comfortable. I personally have respect for each of you. I know that no one meant to hurt anyone else because each of the presenters was very surprised. The whole thing started out with the best intentions and, regardless of what happened, the outcome was probably for the best. I can't believe that this is our last meeting. Although what we've just been through was uncomfortable, to me the whole year has probably been my biggest learning situation.

Silence and different levels of tension permeated the room. Some had come to the conversation at ease and eager to move on, others were passionately concerned with processing what had happened with the group, still others had no strong feelings either way. The discussion continued, with additional members sharing thoughts and some members choosing to remain silent. No longer was the issue only multiculturalism; we were again discussing the responsibility of each member to the group and, not surprisingly, what it meant to be a teacher.

Rosario: I remember that with the first reading in Davis [1990] that he said there were things that were just too personal to teach. That brought trouble. We have to learn to understand feelings and to be dealing with them all the time. Our feelings, students' feelings — these are part of the total atmosphere. I always thought that would only complicate matters and that one should be separated . . . although I found bits of me always squirting out. Teaching means dealing with feelings, and we've learned that it's much more complicated than we first thought.

With that simple statement, Rosario put into words the complex lesson that many of us had learned during these last weeks. Teaching means dealing with feelings, respect, trust, misjudgment, best intentions, and more. That's more complicated than we first thought. We were a group of fourteen people, each with different beliefs, cares, and feelings about what was important in education. At the beginning of our seminar, we encountered significant bumps on the road to planning our year. We struggled with ambiguity, confusion, scheduling, decision making, and the group dynamics present within our learning situation. We learned that we weren't going to be able to satisfy everyone's desired course of study, but we eventually worked out a curriculum with no one leaving the group or seeking out another road. By the end of our seminar we had made a lot of discoveries about teaching, including the discovery that for all that we had been through together, we were still fourteen people, with very different and complex sets of thoughts and feelings.

As we carefully went about the work of mending any remaining hurt feelings and repairing loose ends, our evening of reflection shed light on the fact that teaching can involve pain. Pain is valuable in that it prompts us to stop and look closely. Misunderstanding may result from even the most carefully planned lessons. Hurt feelings may momentarily dash high hopes. Here, at the conclusion of our year together, we felt the pain of learning from our mistakes, of thinking how we might do things differently given a "next time." Strained vision became insight through the passage of time and through eyes that were now willing to see more.

Our discussion was interrupted by a candlelit birthday cake and a chorus of "Happy Birthday, Dear Elissa." Almost instantly the African musical instruments displayed on Eleanor's living room wall somehow ended up in our hands. What resulted was a cacophony of sound, which penetrated the silence and dispersed the tension that had previously filled the room. We were reminded, with each drumbeat and peep from the pipehorn, that we were there to celebrate—Elissa's birthday and our year together.

Two thoughts help to encapsulate our year together. The first is Rosario's concluding thought on this, our final evening: "Although what we've just been through was uncomfortable, to me the whole year has been my biggest learning situation." At one time or another, we had *all* been uncomfortable. And yet for most of us, our time together in ETP had been our "biggest learning situation" of the year. The second thought comes from the Latin phrase *Finis origine pendet*, which Doug, our resident Latin teacher, would probably translate as, "The end depends on the beginning." We began our year by listening to our stories about how we got into teaching. We ended by listening to stories about how we were returning to teaching.

Each of us would be starting out, once again, on our own bumpy road. No longer would we be traveling as a group. Individually we carried with us the lessons we had learned, the many questions left unanswered, a sense of accomplishment, but also a sense of loss. We were again driving by ourselves, still without seatbelts, traversing the bumpy yet wonder-full road of teaching and learning.

Fourteen Teachers Today

Burry Gowen is currently teaching sixth-grade social studies at the Diamond Middle School in Lexington, Massachusetts.

Chris Whitbeck continues teaching seventh- and eighth-grade science at the Lincoln School in Brookline, Massachusetts.

Doug Jones still teaches high school math and Latin at the Buckingham, Browne and Nichols School in Cambridge, Massachusetts, where he is now also an administrator.

Duane Grobman is currently a doctoral student in Teaching, Curriculum and Learning Environments at Harvard Graduate School of Education.

Eleanor Duckworth is still Professor of Education at Harvard Graduate School of Education.

Elissa Wolf is teaching eighth and eleventh grade at Green Farms Academy in Green Farms, Connecticut.

Jane Kays teaches third grade at the Mozart School in Boston, Massachusetts.

Jorge Mejia teaches mathematics at Bogotá's Santa Maria School, where he is chairman of the science and mathematics department.

Kris Newton continues to teach high school physics and general science at Cambridge Rindge and Latin School in Cambridge, Massachusetts, where she is now also a staff developer.

Mark Schoeffel teaches history at the Lawrenceville School in Lawrenceville, New Jersey.

Rosario Jaramillo teaches teachers and does research on adolescents' understanding of history, in Bogotá, Colombia.

Susan McCray is teaching middle school humanities at the Graham and Parks School in Cambridge, Massachusetts.

Suzy Ort is a doctoral student at Teachers College, Columbia University, in New York City.

Tracey Guth is teaching history at Hanover High School in Hanover, Massachusetts.

References

Bailey, T. (1989). *Changes in the nature and structure of work: Implications for skill requirements and skill formation* (Technical Paper No. 9). New York: National Center on Education and Employment, Teachers College, Columbia University.

Banks, J. A. (1977). *Multiethnic education: Practices and promises.* Bloomington, IN: Phi Delta Kappa Educational Foundation.

Bateman, W. (1990). *Open to question: The art of teaching and learning by inquiry.* San Francisco: Jossey Bass.

Boyer, E. (1983). *High school.* New York: Harper & Row.

Brice-Heath, S. (1983). *Ways with words: Language, life and work in communities and classrooms.* New York: Cambridge University Press.

Carnevale, A. P., Gainer, L. J., & Meltzer, A. S. (1989). *Workplace basics: The skills employers want.* Alexandria, VA: American Society for Training and Development.

Darling-Hammond, L. (1990). Achieving our goals: Superficial or structural reforms. *Phi Delta Kappan, 72*(4), 286–295.

Darling-Hammond, L. (1991). The implications of testing policy for educational quality and equality. *Phi Delta Kappan, 73*(3), 220–225.

Darling-Hammond, L., & Wise, A. E. (1985). Beyond standardization: State standards and school improvement. *Elementary School Journal, 85*(3), 315–336.

Davis, B. (1990). *What our high schools could be . . . : A teacher's reflections from the 60's to the 90's.* Toronto: Our Schools/Our Selves Education Foundation and Garamond Press.

Delpit, L. (1988, August). The silenced dialogue: Power and pedagogy in educating other people's children. *Harvard Educational Review, 58*(3), 280–298.

Duckworth, E. (1987). *"The having of wonderful ideas" and other essays on teaching and learning.* New York: Teachers College Press. (2nd edition published 1996)

Escalante, J., & Dirmann, J. (1990). The Jaime Escalante math program. *The Journal of Negro Education, 59*(3), 407–423.

Evans, C., Stubbs, M., Duckworth, E., & Davis, C. (1981). *Teacher-initated research: Professional development for teachers and a method for designing research based on practice.* Cambridge: Technical Educational Research Center.

Freire, P. (1985). *The politics of education: Culture, power and liberation* (D. Macedo, Trans.). South Hadley, MA: Bergin & Garvey.

Greene, M. (1993). Diversity and inclusion: Toward a curriculum for human beings. *Teachers College Record, 95*(2), 211–221.

Hawkins, D. (1974). *The informed vision: Essays on learning and human nature.* New York: Agathon.

Hill, D. (1994, April). Jaime Escalante's second act. *Teacher Magazine*, 23–25.

Hilliard, A. (1994). Misunderstanding and testing intelligence. In J. I. Goodlad & P. Keating (Eds.), *Access to knowledge: The continuing agenda for our nation's schools* (pp. 145–157). New York: The College Board.

Koretz, D. M., Linn, R. L., Dunbar, S. B., & Shepard, L. A. (1991, April). *The effects of high stakes testing on achievement: Preliminary findings about generalization across tests.* Paper presented at the annual meeting of the American Educational Research Association, Chicago.

Kozol, J. (1991). *Savage inequalities: Children in America's schools.* New York: Brown Publishers.

McCall, N. (1994). *Makes me wanna holler: A young black man in America.* New York: Random House.

McCray, S. (1993). SBHS project discovery class: Curriculum overview. Unpublished paper.

McCray, S. (1996). Making the circle bigger: A journey in the South Bronx. In D. Udall & A. Mednick (Eds.), *Journeys through our classrooms* (pp. 149–161). Dubuque, IA: Kendall-Hunt.

Meier, D. (1988, February). Annual meeting of the North Dakota Study Group, Racine, WI.

Nagibin, Y. (1987). The winter oak. In C. R. Christansen (Ed.), *Teaching and the case method* (pp. 227–231). Boston: Harvard Business School.

Neill, M. (1989, October 30). Standardized tests. *The New York Teacher*, p. 8.

Perkins, D., & Blythe, T. (1994). Putting understanding up front. *Educational Leadership, XXIX*(4), 4–7.

Sadker, M., & Sadker, D. (1995). *Failing at fairness: How schools short-change girls.* New York: Simon & Schuster.

Schön, D. (1983). *The reflective practitioner.* New York: Basic Books.

Sizer, T. R. (1984). *Horace's compromise.* New York: Houghton Mifflin.

Sizer, T. R. (1992). *Horace's school.* New York: Houghton Mifflin.

Index